THE LISTENING BIENNIAL READER, VOL. 2:

INFRALISTENING

EDITED BY REBECCA COLLINS & BRANDON LABELLE

THE LISTENING BIENNIAL READER

VOL. 2:

Infralistening

ERRANT BODIES PRESS, BERLIN

CONTENTS

7
**BRANDON LABELLE
WITH REBECCA COLLINS**
On Infralistening

15
MHAMAD SAFA
Collateral Listening:
Towards an
Acoustemology of
Shockwaves

37
MIGUEL BUENROSTRO
Cosmoaudiciones

55
REBECCA COLLINS
Detectives of the
Invisible: Towards a
Cosmological Listening
Practice or How to
Hear Elusive Particles

73
NANNA HAUGE KRISTENSEN
My Mother's Voice

88
PHOTOGRAPHIC DIARY:
The Listening Biennial,
2023

107
**BRANDON LABELLE
WITH WANDA CANTON**
Acoustic Abolitionism:
Interview
with Wanda Canton

119
HENRY IVRY
Listening to Infrastruc-
ture: Acoustic Circulation
and Black Resistance

131
SARA MIKOLAI
Dance as resonant
doing in the myriad of
constraints

139
LUÍSA SANTOS
Imagining narratives
via care and listening

155
BRANDON LABELLE
Drumming Water –
on Wet Sound

171
JAMES WEBB
A series of personal
questions addressed
to the North Sea

177
MARGARIDA MENDES
Sonic Blind Spots:
Acoustic Research on
the Lower
Mississippi River

189
BIOGRAPHIES

BRANDON LABELLE

WITH REBECCA COLLINS

On Infralistening

The Listening Biennial Reader, vol. 2, has been developed following an edition of The Listening Academy held in Bergen, Norway, in 2022. Bringing together a diverse group of contributing researchers, artists, curators and organizers, to share research, practices and experiences, the Academy emerged as a joyful, enriching gathering full of exciting conversations and new friendships. Held at the recently founded Unfinished Institution, a studio collective housed within a former company building in a changing port district in the city, a range of critical topics and questions were shared over the course of presentations, discussions and meals. These included ways of approaching current crises, from environmental destruction and migration politics to the urgencies around decolonizing knowledge practices and how it is we may better listen to the seemingly insignificant and uneventful. Attention turned to processes of memory work, reanimating existing archives, attuning to the life of water bodies, re-working traditions of dance and sounding critical research in the field of theoretical physics, as well as questions of auditory trauma and the politics of assembly and abolitionism. Numerous ideas and reflections circulated, methodologies folded one over the other, critical theories entangled, feelings and creative passions spilled into collective experiments and testings, all of which tenderly, insightfully underscored the importance listening plays in supporting ways of holding and inhabiting plurality – especially in terms of allowing for messy conjunctions and resonant synergies.

In recalling these vibrant days spent in Bergen, we're led to value listening as a research methodology in itself, which is not necessarily singular or easily captured and summed-up, rather, listening figures as highly influential across methodological activities. Listening greatly adds to how it is one may approach creative materials for example, in the artistic processes that require extremely supple forms of attention so as to learn the languages of matter and how to configure other worlds with things; furthermore, listening is there, aiding in sociological, anthropological, ethnographic work, as one encounters a range of voices, languages, signs and symbols, as well as performances, cultural stagings, ceremonial offerings, and which call for a nuanced listening sensibility. This extends to the area of the care sciences, where tending to the pain of others entails a deeply engaged form of listening; across the practices and knowledges that underpin therapeutic and care work, listening is extremely influential. And listening is present in the seemingly silent, self-reflective moments of critical thinking and writing – in conceptualizing ideas and building narratives, in collating, archiving, compiling and editing materials. These are all territories and activities in which cultivating a listening sensibility, or recognizing it as tacit, becomes enabling.

It is along these multiple lines that we have approached developing and editing the Reader. The individual contributions brought together give critical insight into a range of topics while demonstrating listening's role in supporting ways of working, and which contributes to the depth of research and the creative mobilization of given ideas. What comes forward is a sense for listening's ability to take us into transdisciplinary meeting points and intersectional understandings while opening onto emergent gestures of collaboration and intervention. A politics of listening is therefore not only a question of who or what is heard, but also in how listening engenders critical and creative consciousness, and how it affords ways of going places often obscured by dominant epistemological traditions in which *seeing is believing*. As many of the contributions reveal, an acoustic model of thought and action opens entirely different knowledge practices, which often entails pronounced recognition of the embodied, affective and energetic interweave shaping global, planetary coexistence.

To acknowledge and accentuate these perspectives, we've posited *Infralistening* as a thematic framework for the Reader. These are listenings that perform as research methodologies specifically attuned to sub-phenomenal, vibratory, often hidden or under-considered realities, or that seek to creatively engage with existing knowledges and practices in ways that unsettle established forms: a listening that burrows into the archive, a body of tradition, an existing narrative or social construct. Infralistening follows listening into the below, the molecular and energetic, the infrastructural as well as the repercussive, while also inviting listening on the part of others – inviting us to listen *otherwise*, especially in terms of attending to the seemingly insignificant and uneventful. Infralistening is concerned with the *infraordinary* as Georges Perec was to name it, as those seemingly uneventful scenes that mostly define the matters and meanings of life. As articulated in the essays, reflections and conversations presented here, infralistening also comes full circle, traveling across time and space, and finding in the ordinary all the urgencies of extraordinary or exceptional situations. From recollections of formative listening experiences and the slow flourishing of permaculture practices to the traumas experienced in states of war and incarceration, infralistening spirals over itself, to attend in critical and crucial ways to the forms and forces of life in all their breadth and entangled complexity. Infralistening is positioned as a mode of giving attention to the less-than-apparent, and in doing so lends support to what Dimitris Papadopoulos high lights as *alterontologies,* as those "alternative forms of existence" that emerge in tension with dominant society (D. Papadopoulos, *Experimental Practice: Technoscience, Alterontologies, and More-than-social Movements*, Duke University Press 2018: 3). Consequently, infralistening may upset if not break the defining acoustic norms that mostly govern what or who is heard, and how one can remain sensitive to the above and below of the audible spectrum. By attuning to this extended *onto-acoustic* range we may come to detect the murmurings and vibratory motions, the sudden songs and cosmic signals, the troubling damages and rear-guard movements, and which reveal much about human resilience and flourishing.

We're grateful for the opportunity to gather a dynamic and diverse collection of essays, creative texts and projects, and for the chance to elaborate the original exchanges experienced at the Listening Academy in Bergen. While most of the original participants have contributed to the Reader, we have also extended invitations to additional contributors as a way of fleshing out the overall research. This includes integrating a photographic diary offering glimpses into the activities of the Listening Biennial held in 2023 and its various sited manifestations. As the Listening Academy provides a fertile space for ongoing research and whose energies and insights contribute to the curatorial work of the Biennial, it feels important to highlight this connection and the ways in which discursive, research and learning situations are in dialogue with creative, material actions. We hope in this way to add to current discussions on listening cultures and practices, especially with a view toward fostering holistic approaches.

Personal Note:

I remember first meeting Rebecca Collins in Bergen. I had invited her to participate in the Listening Academy, and she had arrived a day early, which gave us the opportunity to meet for dinner in a casual manner. I picked her up from the hotel and we took a slow walk to a Chinese restaurant I thought she would enjoy. During our walk we eased into a lively conversation – I immediately fell in step with Rebecca, feeling encouraged by her wit, her way of talking which was always close to humor, laughter, a sort of ongoing giddiness. These feelings continued as we sat down for dinner, settling into a more relaxed, quiet exchange. We talked about our individual activities, our biographies, sharing stories as well as ambitions; we talked about music, about food, our favorite places to travel, and family. And we talked about listening, anticipating the coming days. As we left the restaurant and walked back to the hotel, our steps felt a bit freer and more playful, feeling a little intoxicated by the ease and richness of our talk as well as the joy of discovering a new friend.

This was to continue over the next days, as I would pick Rebecca up from the hotel every morning, to share a cab ride to the Academy venue. This gentle ritual also quickly developed into a scene of light conversation, sitting in the back of the cab smiling and laughing, sharing our mutual enthusiasm for how the Academy was evolving, and how much we were enjoying the presence of our fellow participants. Rebecca also gave a lot to the overall proceedings, bringing her critical take, always acute and full of insight, into the room.

Given our exchange while in Bergen, it is no wonder that I reached out to her following the gathering, proposing that we work together on editing a book based on the Academy event. Rebecca responded positively, and like before, we quickly fell into lively conversations about what the book could be and how to harness the overall spirit of the gathering. The days led into weeks, then months, and finally years, as we were in no rush to speed ahead; rather, we corresponded with invited contributors, discussing possible directions and themes, such as infralistening; we received, we collected, we read and we responded, editing along the way, alone and together. Following this lengthy process, we had finally arrived at a final version of the book; this was in the spring of 2024. Rebecca and I had a zoom call in April, when we identified a few last points needing to be adjusted, and we had mapped an outline for our introduction, which we planned to write together. We had also planned to meet again in June, in order to continue to discuss the introduction (I was to work on a first draft in the meantime). I remember writing to Rebecca in early June and wondered why I had not heard from her as the weeks went by. As I wrote again, and still received no answer,

I had a feeling something was not right. I knew she was in the process of permanently relocating to Madrid, as she had received a research grant – she was excited for the support, and for the opportunity to continue her current work. To find out more, I visited the website of the institution where she had been working and I was shocked to discover a statement announcing Rebecca's death.

Since that summer, I have worked on carrying our book project, caring for those final details, and for the introduction. Rebecca gave a lot to working on this book, offering precise editorial input to our contributors, as well as producing her own brilliant essay. I'm truly grateful for having had the opportunity to work with her, to take this journey together, and I'm deeply saddened by her absence (we had also talked about organizing events where we could launch the Reader together with the contributors and original collaborators of the Academy). I'm honored and humbled to be able to carry Rebecca's words, her voice, and her spirit in these pages, offering them as a celebration of Her as well as the potentiality of an auditory, sonic practice which she felt passionately about. Along with the contributors, we dedicate this book to Rebecca, with heartfelt admiration and love.

– Brandon LaBelle, May 2025

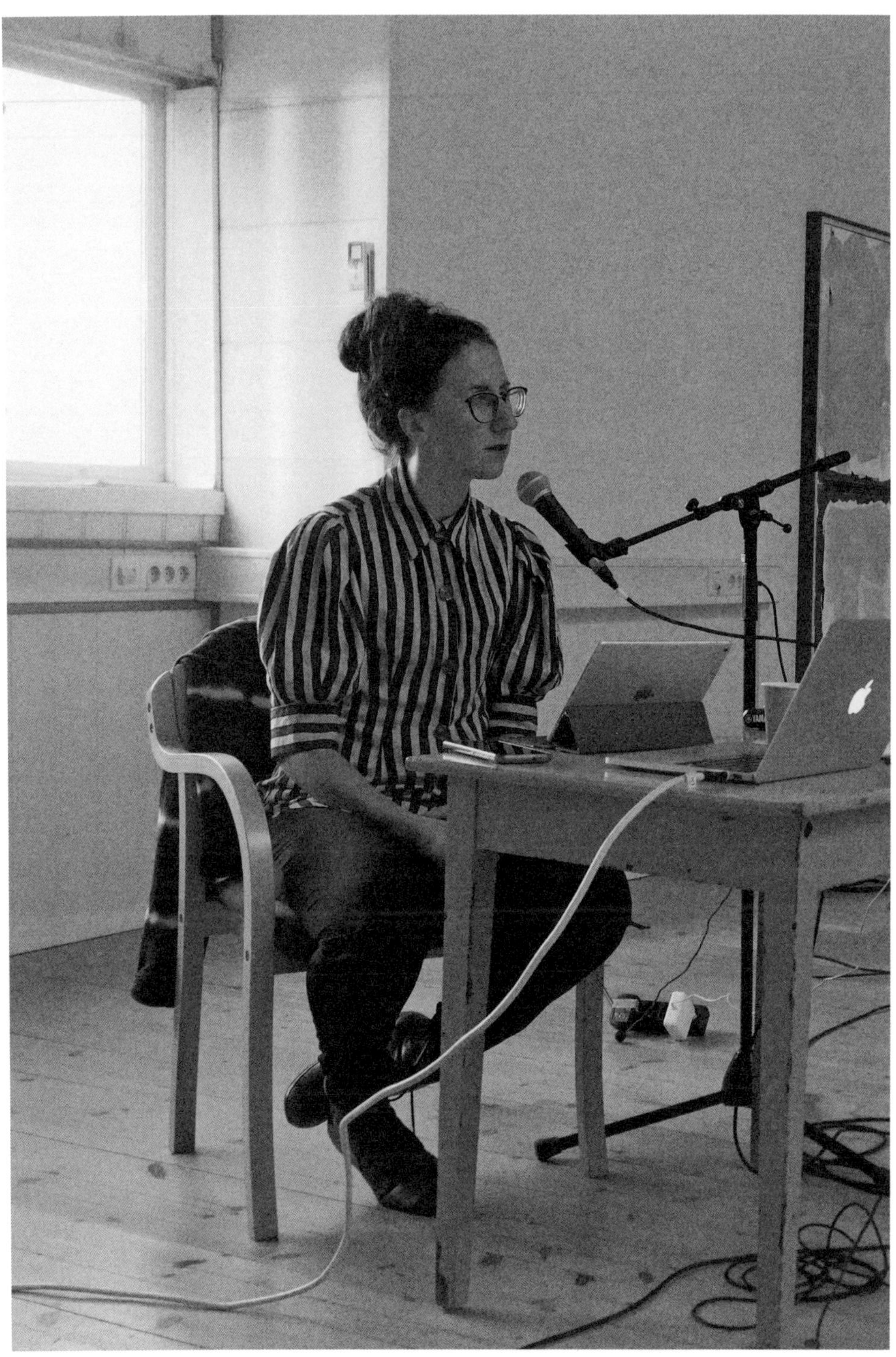

MHAMAD SAFA

Collateral Listening: Towards an Acoustemology of Shockwaves

INTRODUCTION: ON TRAUMA AND THE AUDIBLE BATTLEFIELD

This essay focuses on the impact of military technologies considered "necessary" by belligerents in conflicts despite their unavoidable effects on civilians. It specifically examines the effects of sudden, loud, and blasting sounds during wartime on individuals who are thought to be protected from the effects of military hostilities. Aerial strikes, which are commonly used in contemporary warfare due to their practicality, often result in excessive noise, loud enough to shake civilian infrastructure. Within specific circumstances, these auditory encounters leave lasting impressions on those who experience them. Post-traumatic stress disorder, which is often given less attention in the hierarchy of civilian damage in conflict zones, refers here to the trauma that arises from encounters on the battlefield that overwhelm a person's coping mechanisms. However, hostilities are also a sonorous phenomenon with sound forces arising from various military technologies. The upsurge of long-range ballistics and their subsequent shockwaves gave rise to the unseen symptoms of war that can later resurface as psychological trauma.

I argue that listening to these blasts is a form of "collateral damage". This concept, collateral damage, is articulated within International Humanitarian Law (IHL). This is also known as the law of armed conflict. It functions as a legal framework to regulate the permissible level of violence during conflicts and governs the subsequent military agreements between neo-colonial powers. Within this framework, collateral or incidental damage is a category that arbitrates the amount of tolerated civilian death or damage following so-called legitimate military operations. My hypothesis expands on artist and researcher Susan Schuppli's prompt while she examines the sonic and psychological effects of drone warfare. Schuppli asks:

> At what point is a sound event, one that is the by-product of a specific military technology, deemed sufficiently harmful to count as collateral damage? If its side effects are known, does the continued use of the technology constitute a form of legal liability? (2020, p. 128)

This argument calls into question the impartiality of laws by exploring the relationship between listening and psychological trauma. The relationship between cause and effect is non-linear. This occurs, not only in the realm of law, but also in the fields of acoustics, psychiatry, neuroscience, and their intersection in psychoacoustics. To fully grasp aural traumas, one must draw upon many fields and theoretical frameworks that reach beyond the traditional, so-called rational scientific epistemologies. A paradigm of fear and terror, where sound pressure levels and their vibrations are maximized, can be transformed into an enigmatic one that surpasses logic and scientific reasoning as we know it. Hence this essay foregrounds Collateral Listening and its intertwined themes as an operational concept. Collateral Listening narrates the indiscernible yet instrumentalized techniques and technologies of military violence. A mode of harm that is elusive to law, listening as a form of collateral injury, is not only a critique of the law of armed conflict but also a method that disentangles the mystified causalities of psychological trauma overall.

To unpack this condition, I adopt ethnomusicologist, Steven Feld's concept of acoustemology, where sonic sensibilities are deployed for "making sense, to knowing, to experiential truth" (Feld and Basso, 1996, p. 97). In this sense, witnesses are bound to specific sensory conditions that are singular to their spatial experience of sound. For anthropologist, Marina Peterson, acoustemology, as both a listening and sounding practice is dictated by "sensation, discourse, technology, law and urban infrastructure" (2021, p. 7). My use of acoustemology recognizes the multiple forces shaping the production of knowledge through sonic production and the experience of listening, as grounded within hyper-local conditions. Acoustemology unfolds here through how inhabitants of a land under conflict listen, and the ways in which the perpetrators produce sound.

My approach to shockwave acoustemology is based on video footage taken by civilian witnesses during bombardment and strikes. During the assaults of May 2021 by the Israeli Occupation Forces (IOF) on the besieged Gaza Strip, video recordings of civilians portrayed moments of aerial strikes at night depicting how these were experienced by children in their homes. These live-recorded experiences of violence in Gaza in 2021 are examined as testimonies of an omnipresent and diffused terror. A way to render sounds visible. While closely inspecting these documents, an assemblage of bodily and spatial impacts ensues every strike leaving visible signs of tremors, such as exploding glass. As shockwaves defeat the protective covers of homes and coerce listening subjects fusing them with distant targets, prayers and Quranic recitations emerge as the first expression of shock. Perhaps the resort to the celestial guide is the last remaining shield from the ultimate cataclysmic wave yet to come. In this text, I unpack the (extra)ordinary sonic experience of

Palestinian civilians as Collateral Listening and I consider how a Shockwave Acoustemology is instrumentalized within the bounds of legality during hostilities. Overall, my research offers a contribution to existing studies that attempt to uncover the depth of so-called legitimate military and state violence from its sensorial regimes (Daughtry, 2015; Abu Hamdan, 2018; Schuppli, 2020; Goodman, 2012) where audible and aural faculties are targeted within climates of conflicts.

LESS LETHAL WAR AND LEGAL EVASION

While contemporary warfare is sustained beyond the jurisdictions of neo-colonial powers, the use of force is spread to what is labelled as proxy wars or zones of influence of these powers. As Carl Von Clausewitz famously phrases it, armed conflicts become "the continuation of politics by other means" (1989, p. 87). Since the war between military titans became counter-intuitive and uneconomical following the Second World War, the surge in the influence of the military-industrial complex on political decisions compelled the perpetuation of these hostilities beyond the borders of the global north (Kennedy, 2006, p. 11). These wars are imposed on global-southern nation-states following a dramatic and steep degradation in so-called human rights within territories where extractive ventures have left them with a complete vacuum of wealth and resources. Given these rising, seemingly sporadic pockets of violence, western governments have continuously designed and refined the laws of armed conflict (Jochnick and Normand, 1994) while also exporting them to foreign geographies of conflicts. These laws emerged as a pact among neo-colonial regimes to manage their political relationships, both among themselves and within their former colonies. This same framework had informed as such the "means and methods of combat" (Ibid., p. 68) and the ways in which hostilities should be conducted, performed, and ultimately concluded with a minimal economic, human, and infrastructural cost (Ibid 1994). As the intensities of conflicts fluctuate, the laws are applied among a myriad of international and non-international hostilities.

The case of Palestine unpacks the multidimensional adversities in the application of these laws. It is a geography where all the dysfunctionalities of the laws have converged. Officially considered one of the longest military occupations in modern history under International Humanitarian Law, (Maurer, 2012) asymmetric violence against what remains of the Palestinian territories reconsiders the notions of contemporary conflicts that abide by the legal frameworks. As the recent United Nations report on the status of this occupation portrays, violence is polymorphous, whereby the deliberate traumatization of the indigenous population is indefinable by law (United Nations, 2022). The instrumentalization of what cannot be gauged by the law has taken different and sometimes precise, repetitive trends, such as the deliberate maiming of Palestinian bodies (Puar, 2017), environmental violence in the occupied territories (Isaac and Hilal, 2011; Forensic Architecture, 2014), and also the deployment of Sonic Booms for intimidation (Volcler, 2013; Lieblich, 2014; Parker, 2019; Schuppli, 2020). In this research, I foreground the psycho-social ramification of what is justified as the inexorable effect of the legitimate military operation on the Gaza Strip in the Occupied Territories. Although the causal factors of traumatic stress are diverse in many cases, the colossal sonic surplus that emanates from high-precision aerial strikes elevates the risk of shock among terrorized witnesses.

LEGITIMATE TRAUMAS

On the 10th of May 2021, a military campaign was launched by the Israeli Occupation Forces (IOF) over the besieged Gaza Strip. This operation was preceded by major coercive measures by the occupation forces and settlers alike. These continuous actions attempted to force the expulsion of indigenous Palestinians from the Sheikh Jarrah neighborhood. In addition, the occupation had been conducting raids over the holiest Islamic sites in Jerusalem, Al Aqsa Mosque during one of the most revered nights of the holy month of Ramadan. Faced with a nationwide resistant backlash both from Palestinian civilians and militants, the occupied Gaza Strip had endured a brutal, yet swift assault by the IOF. In a blockaded and fenced 365 km², Gazans had been subjected to eleven days of high-intensity and indiscriminate aerial strikes.

As the televised violence of armed conflicts became prominent following the Vietnam War, public opinion, spectators of war and humanitarian legislators alike have observed the extent of civilian collateral damage as a moral compass for states' military conduct (Crawford, 2013, p. 453). Nonetheless, the media's critical proximity to violence in Gaza not only documented the spectacular ends of military campaigns but also registered its corollary in fear and shock among civilians in the shelters.

Two of the examined videos displayed a common theme. The first video recording depicts children in a residential building reacting to an aerial strike at night. As they get filmed, a bright light accompanied by a blasting sound appears from the window, causing the children to startle in response. A second, even more unsettling video was captured during the day, apparently inside a ground-floor apartment. In this footage, a group of children is seated at the entrance of a shelter, with an elderly man teaching them prayers to ease their fear. As the video captures the explosion a few seconds later, it records the reactions of these children. Seen and heard through these mediated pictorial narratives, sudden loudness, emanating from high-precision strikes, forcefully invades environments that were thought to be spared from the ambivalent list of targets. Extreme sonic repercussions, reverberating the continuum of precise aerial strikes, morph wartime auditors into incidental victims of shockwaves. Listeners to the percussive sonic effects of consecutive blasting are arguably turned, under these conditions, into collateral damage. Such auditory impacts become an engineered assault on bodies located at a threshold between physical injury and critical acoustic intensities that are sufficient to disrupt the state of being of the witness.

While the assessed videos were only two out of many similar ones that have emerged during this short war, they both highlight a category of victim, that is beyond the safeguards of International Humanitarian Law. Those who listen to the intense acoustic aftermath of military operations involuntarily find themselves immersed in the midst of hostilities. The ubiquitous sonic effects of aerial strikes reconfigure the positionality of subjects that are considered hors-de-combat by the laws of armed conflict. These videos visualize the listening habits of war-survivors (or casualties) and push the notion of acoustemology, as discussed in the introduction, to its extreme. Under these conditions, listening and its overwhelming aftereffects become a practice of knowing about the geographies of war and the laws orchestrating them. This acoustemology of violence (Velasco-Pufleau, 2020) offers an account of the residues left by military technologies. It also uncovers the strategies of survival and the spatial particularities of the shelter, the spaces where listeners to war take cover to shield themselves from violence. Within conflicts, acoustemology is a form of knowing about place through listening sensibilities.

However informal, many human-rights-based op-ed articles and research case studies reveal preliminary evidence of post-conflict psychological distress. One scientifically reviewed article only documented the rates of post-traumatic stress disorder (PTSD) among university students in Gaza following the 2021 war. The prevalence of PTSD among 1183 students was stagnant (Radwan et al., 2022). This study, conducted by psychiatrists in Gaza, relied on precise psychiatric and diagnostic methods such as the Impact Event-Scale Revised and the Diagnostic and Statistical Manual for Mental Disorders (DSM). It recounted rates of 88.7 % of severe post-traumatic stress symptoms. However, while assessing the stressors, researchers reached "significant" resulnts where subjects who were not injured or who had not lost a family member also displayed PTSD symptoms. As they discuss these findings, they cite precedents in war-trauma studies among Gazans that found "witnessing the shelling and destruction of other's homes" contributed to 47.4 % of the events that might have contributed to post-traumatic stress (Ibid., p. 11). In addition, they state that "direct intense threats to own safety or safety of beloved ones were reported to be traumatic" (Waller et al., 2012).

By no means as devastating as the killing of 260 Palestinian civilians (Human Rights Watch, 2021), nevertheless, records of clinical post-traumatic stress, re-evaluate and undermine the Israeli military rhetoric that championed their army's adoption of the principles of International Humanitarian

Law. In one of their many legally-coated justifications, the Israeli official's reply to a Human Rights Watch assessment of the legitimacy of their strikes on Gaza in 2021, claimed that

> strikes military targets exclusively, following an assessment that the potential collateral damage resulting from the attack is not excessive in relation to the expected military advantage, ... makes concerted efforts to reduce harm to uninvolved individuals [and] in many of the [May] strikes ... when possible ... provided civilians located within military targets with prior warning (Ibid.).

While recognizing the challenging environment in which the laws of armed conflict function, reassessing the neutrality of these laws necessitates a consideration of the individuals who have encountered the auditory aftermath and the intensity of their resulting symptoms. In order to comprehend the strain inherent in the principles of these laws as they pertain to the definition of collateral damage, and my concept of Collateral Listening, I provide a brief outline of the legal definitions of this concept and its interplay with other legal concepts:

Collateral damage is essentially a non-legal terminology that was used in a military context for the first time in 1961 by Thomas Schelling to describe unintentional civilian death and, or injury during warfare (Schelling, 1961). It is the proportion of civilians, their objects, and the combination thereof, that is legally allowed to be killed, destroyed, or injured during active hostilities between armies or armed groups. As political scientist Neta Crawford upholds, collateral damage "reduces the experience of killing to an abstraction" (2013, p. 1). As such, it grants an elastic threshold to violence and devastation during active hostilities. The laws of armed conflict hinge on collateral damage through one of the law's main guiding principles: the principle of proportionality. Using the term "incidental" instead, Article 51(5)(b) of Additional Protocol I of the Geneva Conventions, in 1977, the principle of proportionality is framed as:

> Launching an attack which may be expected to cause incidental loss of
> civilian life, injury to civilians, damage to civilian objects, or a combi-
> nation thereof, which would be excessive about the concrete and direct
> military advantage anticipated, is prohibited.

Various conventions and prohibitions would later be bound to proportionality as a rationale to circumscribe the effects of warfare on civilians, their objects, and the environment (Solis, 2010, p. 274). As a foundational component of the principle of proportionality, collateral damage is the direct translation of war's devastation. Incidental death and injury are calculated and estimated, setting the scene for unforeseen accidents and technological dysfunctions. Neta Crawford nuances these aspects of collateral damage by separating the "Genuine Accident" from the "systemic" type of collateral damage (2013, p. 8). The latter, in Crawford's analysis, are not unforeseen and unpreventable, given the sophisticated prediction and estimation algorithms used to compute collateral damage radii and discern the crater's circumference of a weapon (Ibid., p. 9).

Since the First World War, and the invention of long-range ballistics, devastation from hostilities have leaked beyond the physical and anatomic realms (Young, 1995; Hecker, 2014). Symptoms from the battlefield, such as shell shock and traumatic neurosis, emerged among combatants who were in close proximity to explosions (Young, 1995; Jones and Wessely, 2005; Fassin and Rechtman, 2009). Besides physical non-lethal injury, grief, displacement, exposure to visible brutality and its ensuing fright, listening to military violence surfaces in this context as a main, inescapable, and pervasive state of contact with combat. When the long-lasting psycho-social effects of military operations are evaluated, the loud and far-reaching sonic impacts become collateral damage for those who hear them. If collateral damage encompasses harm and injury to civilian life resulting from both unforeseeable and permissible effects of military operations, defining the perception of such impacts reconfigures the law's neutrality.

The protection of civilians from the intentional harms of psychogenic nature is raised and observed within sources in international humanitarian law such as article 51(2) of the additional protocol I to the Geneva Conventions. This article prohibits the "acts or threats of violence the primary purpose of which is to spread terror" (Knuckey et al., 2020, pp. 369 – 373). However, the unintentional, incidental side poses several complications to the internal structures of the law of armed conflict (Lieblich, 2014). In short, as legal scholars who have delved into this subject matter convey, the main impediment that prevents psychological damage from being gauged as incidental damage is the difficulty in discerning, measuring and quantifying the stressor (Lieblich, 2014; Knuckey et al., 2020). Among numerous other legal obstacles, this particular angle assumes a certain impossibility in foreseeing the cognitive injury that follows a military operation. Even when the stressor is restricted to a sonic event, one might suppose that its measurability is theoretically established. The conduct of long-range acoustics, especially those accompanying shockwaves, can be so unconventional that it is often difficult to predict (Hecker, 2014, p. 188). Even when using precise prediction technology, such as computational fluid dynamics, a traumatic shock is not a mere result of acoustic parameters.

The subsequent sections of this essay elaborate on how the correlation between listening and psychological trauma does not arise from acoustical attributes defined by scientific and numerical means. In this sense, Collateral Listening is not confined to extreme sound intensity levels, an invasive frequency or spectrum, harmonics, or timbers, but rather takes shape within an entangled condition that acts as scaffolding to sonic effects. This condition is dictated by assemblages of acoustic, spatial, psycho-social, epistemic, and ontological narratives, underpinning the sonic atmospheres of shockwaves.

COLLATERAL LISTENING AT THE EDGES OF FATALITY

Collateral Listening occurs in relation to incidences of violence and requires an altered definition of potentialities, and outcomes. It is different to how listening is defined by Pierre Schaffer as "apprehending something or someone causing a sound in the context of the events" as cited by Tuuri and Eerola (2012, p. 139).

Instead, Collateral Listening becomes a practice of witnessing events which impose an irreversible impact on the witness. This definition of listening and its repercussions are indispensable within violent encounters, as it guides the listener to foresee and locate violence within their vicinity. It is an epistemological practice for locating death, injury, or destruction within one's proximity. Hence, it is vital for survival from these encounters. This mode of listening is also essential as it becomes a practice of knowing in contexts of danger. However, it is the extra-aural, long-lasting, and slowly unfolding effects on the listening subjects that turn this aural experience into a pathogenic one. It is through these conditions and parameters that listening becomes a collateral effect of a sound-emitting source, of an ongoing trauma.

Collateral Listening is where sound is perceived as subordinate to the main intentions of the sounding event. But also, an effect of the primary intentions of an event or an action. Effects such as shock, fear, hopelessness, heightened sensitivity, panic and above all a total dismantling of coping mechanisms. In the context of a blast deriving from an aerial assault, sounds become equipped with the longest propagation capacities, enough to reach and vibrate within the bodies of remote listeners. Collateral Listening is a mode of witnessing the presence of death. The anticipation of the survivor's own demise unfolds as emblematic of the formation and causality of a traumatic experience as psychiatrist Robert Jay Lifton upholds (Caruth and Lifton, 1995). Not limited to armed conflicts, Collateral Listening unfolds whenever an incident manifests itself in sonorous forms that have the capacity to disturb a witness. Essentially, the disturbance occurs whenever the witnesses are incapable of shielding themselves from the invasive powers of the external stressor. As criminologist Juliet Rogers, in her research on the trauma of sexual assault, conveys

> Sound also does not obey the limits of skin – or of rights – and, as such, its evocative presence can resemble the traumatic rupture of the assault itself. The very incapacity to control the borders of the body can feel reminiscent of the invasive experience because sound is not impacted by the "no" (2020, p. 470).

The listener as a witnessing subject is a legal subject and, in singular conditions, should be considered as collateral damage. Sound studies scholar Martin Daughtry's contributions to listening within environments of armed conflict attend indirectly to the collateral listening subject. He espouses the term "auditors" rather than listeners and defines this as "Someone who is within earshot of a sound; also, someone who has the right to hold others accountable for their actions, and for the sensory consequences of those actions" (2015, p. 321). Undoubtedly, the listener is a subject over whom the rules of evidence of criminal proceedings should apply. The subject's testimony is seminal for the overall course of a criminal case. Moreover, the witness' aural condition and the psycho-social one must become a matter of legal scrutiny. In this context, the collateral part of listening, whether it is of a physiological or psychological nature, weighs the legitimacy of any act from which sonic excess is deemed shocking.

RANGE OF COLLATERAL LISTENING

In the aforementioned video documents of May 2021, wartime acoustics are spatially reconfigured. Following every strike there are shakes. Visual signs of extreme distress resonate with the vibrations that invade shelters. As windows shatter, curtains blow and pulverized rubble penetrates homes, torture-like bodily reactions become evidence for the nature of the stressor. Though targets are within distances that were pre-calculated in control rooms to minimize the number of civilian casualties in conformity, in line with the law of armed conflict, bodies that are within tenths, or even hundreds, of meters away absorb the acoustic energies of aerial strikes. Ears and bodies are subjugated to the potential impact of sound as it travels at great distances, infiltrating microscopic porosities while keeping its power and omnipresence. These multidirectional sonic invasions contort the definitions of contact with a threat. Under collateral listening, coercion is pushed to its limits where escape, shelter, and overall protection become futile. Killing as such is sonically transported from the target's coordinates to the witnesses' ears as the blasting waves tremble surrounding architectures, generating an audible atmosphere of terror. An environment whose acoustic signatures would imprint the listeners' construct of fear for years afterwards while depriving them of the possibility of reconciliation with memory. These sonic registers cause ongoing traumas within a geography of sustained violence.

The architecture of homes, underground shelters, rooms, and corridors are incorporated into Collateral Listening. To speak of the range of Collateral Listening is to think of the spatial configuration where the perception of a sonic phenomenon is included within the collateral effects of the emitting source. Within the conflict zone, the sonic atmosphere hegemonized by the resonance of shockwaves is also normalized as an ordinary soundscape of the city. By atmosphere, I refer to law scholar and practicing artist Andreas Philippopoulos-Mihalopoulos's conceptualization of the term. It departs from his concept of the lawscape as the spatial materialization and mattering of law. An atmosphere is where the lawscape withdraws following its intensification. The atmosphere is thus "a space of conflict brimming with ideological charge, aggression, confrontation" (Philippopoulos-Mihalopoulos, 2015, p. 108). Hence, the range of Collateral Listening describes an area where the laws of war are saturated, observed and negotiated. Within this range, legitimate targets and their collateral damage are premeditated, calculated and instrumentalized. These military-legal operations generate a taxonomy of collateral subjects. The killed, and the wounded. Among these injured civilians, an anthology of wounds encompasses the loss of limbs and scarring; the disorders of aural nature, such as permanent hearing damage, tinnitus, the temporary shift in the hearing threshold; and finally, issues of neurological and psychological nature. As the psychopathological damage unfolds typically next to physical injuries, the range of collateral audibility is an inherently unmappable space, that crosses several geographies of conflict. Beyond lethal zones, a collateral range expands as far as the shockwaves can travel whilst keeping their haptic and audible energy. This range materializes through entangled conditions that grant sounds and their vibration the force to travel, resonate, affect, and influence remote subjects. These entanglements encompass a set of atmospheric parameters, namely the environmental ones such as air pressure, and temperature; the infrastructural, architectural and acoustic counterparts such as the absorption coefficients, material densities, shapes and arrangements, resonant frequencies of units, spaces and objects, as well as the number of bodies within a given location; and finally, the psychosocial predisposition of civilians as well as their instantaneous emotional reactivities afforded by the totality of these entanglements during strikes. Marina Peterson describes the entanglement between bodies, sound, and atmospheres, as atmospheric entanglement. Used as a framework to unpack the emergence of noise pollution, Peterson defines her use of the atmospheric as a method which "emphasizes sensation and immaterial forms of energy, materializations over materiality – motion, emergence, immanence, in and of air and sense" (Peterson, 2021, p. 9). It is through these entangled processes that listening, its modes of affect and embodied experience come into being. This atmospheric entanglement is at the basis of any spatial-acoustic cognition within the range of Collateral Listening.

The conditions of listening within this range can become increasingly traumatic whenever coping mechanisms are entirely dismantled. Listening is heavily influenced by the intersection of acoustics, space, and bodies that constitute the dominant atmospheric entanglements. It is through these conjunctions that listening can compute the distances, locations, and directions of potential threats, such as the ones echoing aerial strikes. Yet, threats communicated through acoustic perception are omnidirectional within this range of audibility. The omnidirectionality is narrowed down to the primary acoustic characteristics of long-range acoustic propagation and is, primarily, a non-localizable one.

In situations of extreme listening, where pinpointing the source of a life-threatening event becomes impossible, our survival mechanisms falter. Historically, our ability to locate danger through sound has been a crucial evolutionary asset (Heffner and Heffner 1992; O'Shaughnessy 2009, 125). Therefore, when this capability is impaired, it can profoundly unsettle the listener, thrusting them into unfamiliar terrain. By way of example, during fieldwork for a previous project, I examined the effects of the 2006 war on Lebanon. I interviewed several witnesses about their sonic experience of war. Many of them consistently expressed an inability to identify the exact origin of a blast when questioned about its location. This uncertainty intensified their feelings of fear. As Witness "S" vividly described, "The sheer intensity of the sound was so overwhelming that I found myself wishing a building would collapse just to identify the source of the noise." Similarly, Witness "Y" contrasted her experience of strikes with that of car bombs she had previously encountered: "Strikes felt more distant yet immense. They seemed indiscriminate, engulfing everything around, whereas, with a car bomb, I could discern its location more accurately." When I questioned witness "J" about his ability to discern the direction of artillery fire and the strikes he observed during the war, he responded, "I couldn't really tell. My immediate reaction was to quickly find refuge, usually ducking under a random table in the house."

The interaural time and intensity difference phenomenon determines a sound source's localization. This involves a differential equation in which the ears calculate the time it takes for a sound to reach each ear and the differences in sound level between them. When sounds are emitted within the horizontal plane of the ears, the interaural time difference process applies automatically to low frequencies, while the interaural intensity difference process applies to high frequencies (Schnupp, Nelken and King, 2011, pp. 210 – 219; Bear, Connors and Paradiso, 2016, pp. 395 – 398). However, the process of sound localization becomes more complicated when the lowest frequencies are radiated vertically, rendering it ineffective. As a result, the long-range propagation of aerial strikes, within which the lowest frequencies travel the furthest, obstruct localization. This is due to the sound reflections (Schnupp, Nelken and King, 2011, p. 219), omnidirectionality (a blend of vertical and horizontal sound reflections), and the prolonged sound duration that continues for several seconds after the initial impact. Within this atmosphere hearing is stripped of its ability to localize sounds, making it impossible to accurately identify the source of a sound (Daughtry, 2015, p. 202). In this context, trauma is defined as an increased perception of threat, which is primarily non-localizable. As a result, the geography of trauma is difficult to map and pinpoint (Coddington and Micieli-Voutsinas, 2017).

On the 20th of May 2021, hostilities ceased between the Israeli occupation forces and the Palestinian armed factions in Gaza. During these eleven days of high-intensity military confrontations, 1,500 aerial strikes were conducted over Gaza (Robinson and Overton, 2021) in response to Hamas' rockets that were predominately intercepted by Israel's "Iron Dome." International human rights groups, as well as some states' representatives, called for an investigation, known sometimes as post-ex identification, to unveil possible violations of the laws of armed conflicts from both sides of the conflict. The International Criminal Court initiated an inquiry over alleged war crimes, unlawful targeting and other misuse of force by "both sides" of the conflict (Human Rights Watch, 2021). The aftermath of these aerial strikes, which are considered "high precision" have both fatal and non-fatal consequences. These include sonic disturbances, which require a reconsideration of the type of damage caused by these operations, particularly when they are carried out at a frequency of 136 strikes per day. At this rate, the daily aural experiences of Palestinian civilians were saturated with vibrational and elevated sound pressure levels, given the compact size of the besieged Gaza Strip. Although there is a lack of all-inclusive and detailed psychiatric research conducted after the Gaza war in May 2021, a collection of records from previous years (Baker and Shalhoub-Kevorkian, 1999; Thabet and Thabet, 2017; Manzanero et al., 2021) highlights a group of victims who are not acknowledged under the law of armed conflict. Yet, the prevailing atmospheric entanglement in warfare geographies narrates the extent of traumatic stress inflicted, despite the presence of multiple factors contributing to its cause.

In what I refer to as the range of collateral listening, the shockwave resulting from an aerial strike acts as a dominant external force that gives rise to information and narratives on bodies, subjectivities, laws, and military technologies in the affected environments. By listening to and sensing shockwaves new beings emerge: the shellshocked, hysteric, neurotic, traumatized and the ones suffering from concussion. As a result, shockwaves are both an ontological and epistemic phenomenon. An ontological definition of shockwaves is derived from multiple perspectives (Goodman, 2012). Nevertheless, when new subjectivities and pathologies materialize on the battlefield, shockwave ontologies come to matter within a precise set of conditions. These are informed by distances, scales, types of ammunition, proximity to civilian infrastructures and the intensity by which these are applied. Ontology here is a matter of relationality between all these elements, whereby the scope and breadth of its action are altered along these parameters.

Equally, the epistemic nature of shockwaves are not strangers to military contexts. Sonic sources propagate within a continuum of mediums before they get sensed by an apparatus, such as radar, an antenna, a microphone or in this case an ear. Shockwaves, through audible and vibrational dynamism, drive these apparatuses to their extremes. They echo the technologies operating during conflicts, but also a generation of pathologies as well as their diagnostic tools. Sensing, listening and analyzing shockwaves and their sonorous outcomes is an epistemology of the nature of violence. The collateral listening that the auditors of these military campaigns compromise is an assemblage of actions that go beyond the immediacy of a mere hearing experience. As shockwaves become regular within these territories, they lose their extraordinary dimension. By means of auditory and tactile patterns, social infrastructures and relationalities between the listeners, the therapeutic institutions, and the laws governing the status of the non-combatant are normalized. These established norms directly translate into corporeal yet legally evasive encounters with violence. These are reflective of the geopolitical priorities that actively marginalized the Palestinian subject. Applying Feld's methodological approach to acoustemology enables a process of knowing through the causalities and effects of shockwaves. This approach reveals the agencies that are responsible for creating the network of actions that enable listening. Through acoustemology, the constituents of listening assemblages, or agencies, become evident. Ultimately, this reading enables a deeper discourse on accountability within the frameworks of law. As Karen Barad conveys:

... responsibility, and accountability take on entirely new valences. There are no singular causes. And there are no individual agents of change. Responsibility is not ours alone. And yet our responsibility is greater than it would be if it were ours alone. Responsibility entails an ongoing responsiveness to the entanglements of self and other, here and there, now and then. (2007, p. 394)

NOTES

1. A sonic boom is a phenomenon in aerodynamics and physics that occurs when an aircraft flies at supersonic speed and generates a shockwave.

2. https://www.aljazeera.com/opinions/2021/6/14/trauma-and-mental-health-in-gaza (accessed 02 /11/2023)
   https://reliefweb.int/report/occupied-palestinian-territory/gaza-wounds-dont-heal (accessed 01/11/2023)
   https://www.reuters.com/world/middle-east/some-gaza-children-another-round-violence-reopens-trauma-2022-08-18/ (accessed 01/11/2023)
   https://www.al-monitor.com/originals/2021/06/gaza-children-deal-psychological-trauma-month-after-war (accessed 04/11/2023)

3. The DSM is a widely adopted manual that categorizes the different types of psychiatric disorders. Now in its 5th revised version, it was initially designed, published, and adopted in 1952 and constantly revised by the American Psychiatric Association. Although widely criticized for its non-inclusive dimension, yet it remained the most comprehensive and referenced document for psychiatric diagnosis. Several measurement methods are applied to verify the diagnostic criteria of the DSM, namely, to assess the severity of Post-Traumatic Stress Disorder. The Impact Event Scale is one of these measurement techniques that quantifies the subjective nature of distress following the exposure to a traumatic stressor.
   Additional Protocol I, Article 51(5)(b) (adopted by 77 votes in favour, one against and 16 abstentions) (cited in Vol. II, Ch. 4, § 1) and Article 57(2)(a)(iii) (adopted by 90 votes in favour, none against and 4 abstentions) (cited in Vol. II, Ch. 5, § 325).
   https://www.reuters.com/world/middle-east/israels-gaza-challenge-stopping-metal-tubes-turning-into-rockets-2021-05-23/ (Accessed 01/11/2023).

Abu Hamdan, L. (2018) 'Aural Contract: Investigations at the Threshold of Audibility'. Available at: https://doi.org/10.25602/GOLD.00023293.

Baker, A. and Shalhoub-Kevorkian, N. (1999) 'Effects of political and military traumas on children The palestinian case', *Clinical Psychology Review*, 19(8), pp. 935 – 950. Available at: https://doi.org/10.1016/S0272-7358(99)00004-5.

Barad, K. M. (2007) *Meeting the universe halfway: quantum physics and the entanglement of matter and meaning*. Durham: Duke University Press.

Bear, M. F., Connors, B. W. and Paradiso, M.A. (2016) *Neuroscience: exploring the brain*. Enhanced fourth edition. Burlington, MA: Jones & Bartlett Learning.

Caruth, C. and Lifton, R. J. (1995) 'An Interview with Robert Jay Lifton', in *Trauma: explorations in memory*. Baltimore: Johns Hopkins University Press.

Clausewitz, C. von (1989) *On war*. First paperback printing. Princeton, N.J: Princeton University Press.

Coddington, K. and Micieli-Voutsinas, J. (2017) 'On trauma, geography, and mobility: Towards geographies of trauma', *Emotion, Space and Society*, 24, pp. 52 – 56. Available at: https://doi.org/10.1016/j.emospa.2017.03.005.

Crawford, N. (2013) *Accountability for killing: moral responsibility for collateral damage in America's post-9/11 wars*. Oxford: Oxford University Press.

Cusick, S. G. (2008) '"You are in a place that is out of the world …": Music in the Detention Camps of the "Global War on Terror"', *Journal of the Society for American Music*, 2(01). Available at: https://doi.org/10.1017/S1752196308080012.

Daughtry, J. M. (2015) *Listening to war: sound, music, trauma and survival in wartime Iraq*. New York: Oxford University Press.

Fassin, D. and Rechtman, R. (2009) *The Empire of Trauma: An Inquiry Into the Condition of Victimhood*. Princeton University Press.

Feld, S. and Basso, K.H. (eds) (1996) *Senses of place*. 1st ed. Santa Fe, N.M. : [Seattle]: School of American Research Press ; Distributed by the University of Washington Press (School of American Research advanced seminar series).

Fisher, J. P. and Flota, B. (eds) (2011) *The politics of post-9/11 music: sound, trauma, and the music industry in the time of terror*. Farnham, Surrey, England ; Burlington, VT: Ashgate Pub (Ashgate popular and folk music series).

Forensic Architecture (2014) *Herbicidal Warfare In Gaza* ← Forensic Architecture. Available at: https://forensic-architecture.org/investigation/herbicidal-warfare-in-gaza (Accessed: 1 November 2023).

Goodman, S. (2012) *Sonic warfare: sound, affect, and the ecology of fear*. First MIT Press paperback edition. Cambridge, Mass. London: MIT Press (Technologies of lived abstraction).

Haldeman, J. W. (1974) *The forever war*. London: Gollancz.

Hecker, T. (2014) *The Era of the Megaphonics: On The Productivity of Loud Sound, 1880 – 1930*. McGill University.

Human Rights Watch (2021) 'Gaza: Apparent War Crimes During May Fighting | Human Rights Watch', 27 July. Available at: https://www.hrw.org/news/2021/07/27/gaza-apparent-war-crimes-during-may-fighting (Accessed: 1 November 2023).

Isaac, J. and Hilal, J. (2011) 'Palestinian landscape and the Israeli-Palestinian conflict', *International Journal of Environmental Studies*, 68(4), pp. 413 – 429. Available at: https://doi.org/10.1080/00207233.2011.582700.

Jochnick, C. and Normand, R. (1994) 'The Legitimation of Violence: A Critical History of the Laws of War', in *The Development and Principles of International Humanitarian Law*. 1st edn. Routledge, pp. 49 – 95. Available at: https://doi.org/10.4324/9781315086767-2.

Jones, E. and Wessely, S. (2005) *Shell shock to PTSD: military psychiatry from 1900 to the Gulf War*. Hove; New York: Psychology Press (Maudsley monographs, no. 47).

Kennedy, D. (2006) *Of war and law*. Princeton [N.J.]: Princeton University Press.

Knuckey, S. et al. (2020) 'The Proportionality Rule and Mental Harm in War', in Knuckey, S. et al., *Necessity and Proportionality in International Peace and Security Law*. Oxford University Press, pp. 367 – 408. Available at: https://doi.org/10.1093/oso/9780197537374.003.0013.

LaBelle, B. (2010) *Acoustic territories: sound culture and everyday life*. New York: Continuum.

Lieblich, E. (2014) 'Beyond Life and Limb: Exploring Incidental Mental Harm Under International Humanitarian Law', in D. Jinks, J.N. Maogoto, and S. Solomon (eds) *Applying International Humanitarian Law in Judicial and Quasi-Judicial Bodies*. The Hague: T.M.C. Asser Press, pp. 185 – 218. Available at: https://doi.org/10.1007/978-94-6265-008-4_7.

Manzanero, A. L. et al. (2021) 'Traumatic Events Exposure and Psychological Trauma in Children Victims of War in the Gaza Strip', *Journal of Interpersonal Violence*, 36(3 – 4), pp. 1568 – 1587. Available at: https://doi.org/10.1177/0886260517742911.

Maurer, P. (2012) 'Challenges to international humanitarian law: Israel's occupation policy', *International Review of the Red Cross*, 94(888), pp. 1503 – 1510. Available at: https://doi.org/10.1017/S1816383113000593.

Ouzounian, G. (2020) *Stereophonica: sound and space in science, technology, and the arts*. Cambridge, Massachusetts: The MIT Press.

Papaeti, A. (2020) 'On Music, Torture and Detention: Reflections on Issues of Research and Discipline', *Transposition* [Preprint], (Hors-série 2). Available at: https://doi.org/10.4000/transposition.5289.

Parker, J. E. K. (2019) 'Sonic lawfare: on the jurisprudence of weaponised sound', *Sound Studies*, 5(1), pp. 72 – 96. Available at: https://doi.org/10.1080/20551940.2018.1564458.

Peterson, M. (2021) *Atmospheric noise: the indefinite urbanism of Los Angeles*. Durham: Duke University Press (Elements).

Philippopoulos-Mihalopoulos, A. (2015) *Spatial justice: body, lawscape, atmosphere*. Milton Park, Abingdon, Oxon [UK]; New York, NY: Routledge (Space, materiality, and the normative).

Puar, J.K. (2017) *The Right to Maim: Debility, Capacity, Disability*. Duke University Press. Available at: https://doi.org/10.1215/9780822372530.

Radwan, A.-K. S. et al. (2022) Post-traumatic stress disorder among Palestinian university students following the May 2021 war. preprint. In Review. Available at: https://doi.org/10.21203/rs.3.rs-1483103/v1.

Robinson, S. and Overton, I. (2021) *The targeting of high-rises in Gaza: an analysis of Israel's air strikes on tall buildings in 2021 – occupied Palestinian territory* | ReliefWeb. Available at: https://reliefweb.int/report/occupied-palestinian-territory/targeting-high-rises-gaza-analysis-israel-s-air-strikes-tall (Accessed: 1 November 2023).

Rogers, J. (2020) 'The sound of the perpetrator – thoughts on trauma and voice in Big Little Lies', *Law Text Culture*, (24), pp. 455 – 479.

Schelling, T. C. (1961) 'Dispersal, Deterrence, and Damage', *Operations Research*, 9(3), pp. 363 – 370. Available at: https://doi.org/10.1287/opre.9.3.363.

Schnupp, J., Nelken, I. and King, A. (2011) *Auditory neuroscience: making sense of sound*. Cambridge, Mass: MIT Press.

Schuppli, S. (2020) *Material witness: media, forensics, evidence*. Cambridge, Massachusetts: The MIT Press (Leonardo).

Solis, G. D. (2010) *The law of armed conflict: international humanitarian law in war*. Cambridge, [Eng] ; New York: Cambridge University Press.

Sterne, J. (ed.) (2012) *The sound studies reader*. New York: Routledge.

Thabet, A. A. M. and Thabet, S.S. (2017) 'Coping With Trauma Among Children in South of Gaza Strip', *Psychology and Cognitive Sciences – Open Journal*, 3(2), pp. 36 – 47. Available at: https://doi.org/10.17140/PCSOJ-3-122.

Tuuri, K. and Eerola, T. (2012) 'Formulating a Revised Taxonomy for Modes of Listening', *Journal of New Music Research*, 41(2), pp. 137 – 152. Available at: https://doi.org/10.1080/0929821 5.2011.614951.

United Nations (2022) *Israeli occupation of Palestinian territory illegal: UN rights commission* | UN News. Available at: https://news.un.org/en/story/2022/10/1129722 (Accessed: 1 November 2023).

Velasco-Pufleau, L. (2020) 'Introduction. Sound, Music and Violence', *Transposition* [Preprint], (Hors-série 2). Available at: https://doi.org/10.4000/transposition.5160.

Volcler, J. and Volk, C. (2013) *Extremely loud: sound as a weapon*. New York: The New Press, Distributed by Perseus Distribution.

Young, A. (1995) *The harmony of illusions: inventing post-traumatic stress disorder*. Princeton [N.J.]: Princeton University Press.

MIGUEL BUENROSTRO

Cosmo-audiciones

De la lengua maya aprendieron que
no hay
jerarquía que separe al sujeto
del objeto,
porque yo bebo el agua que me bebe y
soy mirado
por todo lo que miro,
y aprendieron a saludar así:
— Yo soy otro tú.
— Tú eres otro yo.
(Galeano, 2011, p. 97)

To think geo- and body-politically (Mignolo, 2002, p. 274) involves listening to the border, it challenges us to unfix the categories of homeland which are tied to the construction of nationhood. When we unravel the border from national belonging, we move beyond the static geographies and dominant narratives surrounding the topic of migration, a topic often depicted as a violent and racialized experience. While I acknowledge the systemic violence implicated in the journeys of migration, my intent is not to ignore the suffering of people, but rather listen to the histories of people in their pursuit to live a dignified life. Listening to the border involves embracing memory and knowledge relations that converge within the crossroads of national boundaries. When we listen to the implicit memory embedded in testimonies, oral history of musical journeys, we attune to the border. The border becomes a contact zone, a site for exchange that situates oneself in order to move beyond the confines of nationhood, towards re-existence and radical imagination.

During the Covid-19 lockdown, I started to develop a series of sonic interventions across various public spaces in Berlin.[1] This initiative began with my engagement with migrant musicians performing in the city's corridors, tunnels, and subway stations. The lockdown left street musicians with no income, no audience, however while passing through the museum island of Berlin, you could listen to the echoes of different music playing in the empty alleyways. Through numerous dialogues, an artistic exploration emerged – these musicians, who each come from diverse backgrounds, were connected through their musical constellations, shaping their unique perception of Berlin. Amidst these encounters, I had the privilege of conversing with Luis Lincheo, a Mapuche Chilean musician, and Bosnian artist, Stevica Dimic. Listening to their experiences, revealed a profound connection between their personal stories and the music they would play in the alleyways of the Museum Island in Berlin. This immersion allowed me to perceive the border – a source of knowledge – not as a physical barrier but as a sonic dimension, woven into human mobility. Their journeys, memories, and present-day associations with Berlin unfolded through their melodies and recollections.

After witnessing these moments through days of filming across different tunnels beneath the bridges of the Museum Island in Berlin, our performances took shape. In my project and performance series titled *Sonora* (2020) I staged, alongside the aforementioned musicians, improvisational actions. These captivated listeners and casual pedestrians by sparking light and adding sonority to unconventional urban spaces on the Museum Island. Through different cinematic actions, such as light, shadow and the presence of different pedestrians, we brought forth these shared experiences.[2]

It was within the very spaces that often went unnoticed that we showcased these musical memories. In Luis Lincheo's music, I encountered the border within the resonance of his compositions intertwined with his reflections on how North American first nation flutes echo the profound depths of the Andean winds. The solitude of the sound embedded in melodic Oriental traditions was also reflected upon in his storytelling. Stevica Dimic, on the other hand, shared melodies on his accordion. Songs he once played to his daughter, soothing her into peaceful dreams. Before his arrival in Germany, he sold many of his cherished instruments, seeking a better life. The accordion was the only instrument he kept, intertwined with his memories, it carried the border in the form of a deep remembrance of his daughter. These memories, as he played, became embedded in the reverberations of the brick-walled tunnels on Museum Island. Through these journeys of south to north and east to west, I listened to the essence of migration, an experience far removed from the simplistic portrayal depicted by rhetoric of the far right. These encounters gave me the framework to pose questions: What does it mean to listen to the border? How can the act of listening become an alternative to the singular narratives of "otherness" embedded in the process of migration? *Sonora* illuminated the richness of personal stories, resonating far beyond the confines of geographical boundaries or divisive depictions.

Listening can help us gain deeper understanding of the complex journeys of people in movement. When we *listen* to the border, we don't rely on the exploitative images perpetuated by the media, nor do we minimize the understanding of the border through its physical delimitations. Through listening to the border, we can feel the complex interconnectedness of local and global histories that are shaped by difference, expressing the fluid realities in which communities dwell between citizenship and statelessness. The willingness to listen enables us to explore these histories horizontally. This provides the ways in which we do not objectify or commodify the subjectivities of the individuals and communities in the process of migration. By moving away from the dominant narratives, we unfold the border as a site of knowledge production and interconnection. Or, in the words of Chicana feminist scholar Gloria Anzaldúa, as "constant state of transition" (1985, p. 25). The border, in this sense, becomes a point of departure that serves as a contact zone for the diasporas and generations of migrant families around the world.

I am interested in the vital role that music plays in this mobility process as it carries along memories, rhythms, stories that nurture alternative forms of belonging. It is through these musical journeys that I explore the topic of migration. To listen to the border is to listen to those who cross it; *los atravesados / los que atraviesan.*

LISTENING TOGETHER

To build on *Sonora* I developed *Cosmoaudiciones*, a more extensive artistic research project.[3] For this work I collaborated with musicians of migratory background to trace relationships between sound recordings held at the Berlin Phonogramm-Archiv and the musical worlds that travel through the Atlantic into the Caribbean and the Americas.

The Berlin Phonogramm-Archiv was established in 1900 by psychologist Carl Stumpf in order to collect and preserve the phonographic recordings of non-European music. The recordings served as the primary research material for what we understand today as comparative musicology or ethnomusicology. The main premise of this discipline was to "collect as many examples of traditional music as possible, in order to create and follow theories about the origin and evolution of music." (Koch, Wiedmann and Ziegler, 2004, p. 189) The archive was part of a German colonial apparatus in which travelers, ethnologists or colonial officers brought recordings of music and voices to the Berlin Ethnological Museum. Here, the recordings would be classified, studied and preserved alongside collections of artifacts and archaeological pieces. During the initial period of generating the collection, a large number of recordings were gathered in former German colonies, international world fairs and colonial fairs. European powers would display captured bodies in what used to be known as "ethnological expositions", essentially human zoos, where many of these recordings were exhibited. The recordings of the Berlin Phonogramm-Archiv were exhibited for the first time internationally at The Universal Exposition of 1889 (Exposition Universelle) in Paris and then continued to be exhibited along with people from different colonies around the world. The phonograph recordings are powerful statements of the European construction of otherness. Along with looted artifacts, objects and archaeological treasures, these sound collections are housed in sound banks and archives of national museums; where they are now subjected to critical observation, and study regarding the issues of European colonial heritage and questions of restitution.

My aim with *Cosmoaudiciones* is to suggest a way of approaching the sonic materials housed in the Berlin Phonogramm-Archiv through a listening positionality in order to understand them as a constellation of listening relations that can be re-socialized, re-embodied and re-weaved into the music and performativity of everyday life. With this in mind, myself and the other participants, do not claim that we are providing an answer to the enormous absence of histories and violence implicated in museum collections. By re-thinking the archival recordings as relations, we re-inscribe a new set of histories that can take us further than the ethnographic experience of the institutional walls within which they remain.

Over a six-month period, our focus, in the archive, centered on listening to musical recordings spanning diverse territories: from the Mayan peninsula in Mexico to the Andes regions of Bolivia, Peru, and Ecuador, to the Amazon in Brazil, and territories between Colombia and Venezuela. This exploration extended further and was juxtaposed with recordings from West Africa – encompassing what we recognize today as Ghana, Uganda, Congo, Angola, and Zimbabwe.

To initiate listening sessions in the archive I invited Peruvian musician Laura Robles to take part. Laura is an Afro-Peruvian percussionist deeply immersed in a variety of Berlin music scenes. These range from traditional folklore music, to free jazz and experimental music.

Alongside Laura I began to immerse myself into Berlin's musical scene. She introduced me to Trigo Santana, a Brazilian bass player, and Robby Geerken, a percussionist specialized in Caribbean rhythms. Into this ensemble of listeners, I also welcomed Fabiano Lima, a Brazilian ritual musician, and Tom Kessler, a Mexican experimentalist and jazz musician. Together, we delved into sonic materials, playing them repeatedly and exchanging our thoughts and perceptions. Each of us brought forth a rhythm we found compelling from the assigned recordings, engaging these rhythms in dialogue with one another. We practiced and experimented, raising notions about resemblances and synchronicities with other musical spheres. Together we found a vast field of exploration in the imprecise timing found in different music, exemplified in recordings from the Colorado people in Ecuador. We listened to old recordings of Japanese ritual music, featuring gongs, micro string instruments, and winds that resonate musical journeys in the Andes region, and long atmospheres sounding as if time expanded. The errors and clashes of gongs, the flow of music, and the varied tempos that would be imprecise to Western ears, constituted for us a music attuned to its ritualistic context, the materiality and the deep remembrance of earth worlds. These temporalities served as the conceptual framework for our artistic endeavor. Aside from music, we also listened to conversations, soundscapes, and integrated these moments into our discussions.

Throughout this process, our approach evolved into a method of mapping sonic affinities and textures. Our aim was to redefine these rhythms as more than mere sequences and repetitive sounds. We wanted to consider rhythm as a repository of knowledge – encompassing elements of time, space, ritual, emotion, and the fabric of daily life. Our conceptual framework centered on understanding the oceanic exchanges between the Atlantic and the Caribbean and how they were blended across different territories of the Americas. Through the rhythms we found in different recordings, we began to imagine musical journeys, memories and points of encounter between different musical worlds. During our listening periods with the ethnographic collections the following questions served to orientate our thinking:

*How can we perform the archive outside the museum
and into public spaces?*

*How can we restore time from the extracted worlds
of meaning?*

How can we "sound" the archive with dignity?

*How can we re-socialize that which remains
absent from the archive?*

*How can listening practices move us towards
re-futuring musical worlds?*

LISTENING — SENSING — RECEIVING

I first came across the term *Cosmoaudición* (*Cosmoaudition*) when reading Carlos Lenkersdorf's book *Aprender a Escuchar* (*Learning to Listen,* 2008). Lenkersdorf was a German philosopher and linguist living in Mexico after fleeing Germany from the second world war. After teaching philosophy in the Autonomous National University in Mexico, he studied the Maya-Tojolabal language, a language spoken in regions of the southern state of Chiapas. In his writings, Lenkersdorf acknowledges the importance of listening for the Maya peoples, to the extent of understanding "listening" as a central pillar of their political and social system. He used the term *Cosmoaudición* to define a philosophy of listening of the Maya-Tojolabal people. When we understand listening as a philosophy, we can differentiate a *Cosmoaudición* from a *Cosmovisión*; if our Cosmovision is the way we perceive and experience the world through a world view, then our *Cosmoaudición* would refer to the way we experience and understand the world through listening, a "philosophy of listening."

The resonance I felt with this term stems from Lenkersdorf's connection between a philosophy of listening and the study of languages in the south of Mexico. Carlos Lenkersdorf understood how listening aligns us with others, and in this way, "a horizontal structure is established in the realms of the social, cultural, economic, political, and cosmic levels" (Lenkersdorf, 2008 p. 19). This relation became the entry point when translating the Mayan Tojolabal language. As for us, when co-listening to ethnographic recordings, we were aligned with each other, together we would open up a world of sonority, a musical constellation.

It was through the understanding of a shared recognition with others, that we attuned to a *cosmoaudición*. These thoughts guided us through the process of co-listening to the materials of the Berlin Phonogramm-Archiv.

While acknowledging the importance of archiving sonic documents, the listening sessions prompted a deeper reflection on the motivations behind collections and the urgency to demystify musical worlds, sharing its essence with others. Our initial criteria for selecting recordings stemmed from a mutual understanding that our investigation couldn't replicate a nationalist German historiography towards the "primitive other." Hence, we proposed an "ethics of listening" – a means to engage with recordings by sharing the sensory experiences they offered. Delving deeper into rhythmic patterns, affinities and exchanging perceptions, memories and emotions stirred by diverse music guided our exploration.

To be attuned to a *cosmoaudición* involves being aware of the concept of "we." Within the Mayan Tojolabal language, the concept of "we" takes priority over the individual "I," but also functions as a shared recognition in which people are always in relation with their surroundings, understanding themselves collectively. Therefore, listening to sonic materials requires a process of collective listening; all of us would listen to the material together and all of us would share our thoughts, senses and impressions. The materials went from being static documents in museum collections to newly awakened sonic relations, re-circulating in our bodies, soon to be performed in the public realm. When performing the archive, we moved beyond the mere re-interpretation of indigenous music, and we delved into the limitations of approaching sound documents from colonial collections.

An important acknowledgement for us was the absence of Caribbean musical worlds within the archive, it raised an important discussion among us; the absence of phonographic recordings was, in part, due to the quest for "purity" by ethnographers. In their thinking, they often reduced Caribbean music to a simplistic label of "African music," failing to acknowledge its distinct musical lineage and form.

Engaging with the absence enabled us to re-inscribe a sonic imagination beyond the confines of "original music." Instead, we approached the Caribbean as a crucial intersection – a meeting point between plural musical worlds. We facilitated this understanding by jamming along the existing recordings, creating a dynamic interplay generating something similar to a "live sonic documentary" and an expanded archive, where we hosted each other in rhythm.

Our engagement with these varied sonic realms compelled us to question the politics inherent in archiving and the act of subjecting people through colonial practices. Historical recordings often captured instances where colonial officers, travelers, or scientists coerced indigenous communities into performing "original" songs or evoking spiritual rituals. In such recordings, there was a lack of contextual understanding or appreciation for the intricate relationships between these practices of everyday lives amongst the subjected community. For some of us, the music found in the recordings meant ancestral knowledge, memory and points of encounter, to others, the ethnographic recordings bore witness to racial purity and supremacist behavior. The people who were persuaded to "sing original songs" were often referred to as "Indians," they had no name, no history, no humanity. This was the case when we listened to recordings of the Mayan people of Mexico. The recording ethnographer, with no knowledge of Mayan languages, would speak on behalf of his subjects, often deducing their songs to exotic gestures. This act of "Sonic Extraction" mirrored a perverse use of recording technology. It was a means to extract the voices of those relegated to a perceived "primitive" era, soon to be archived as part of the Berlin Phonogramm-Archiv which, at the time, formed part of Berlin's Royal Ethnological Museum. Listening closely we would sense how the ethnographer was fooled by the people. In order to get a quick cash they would randomly sing and performed meaningless slurs to make the ethnographer believe he was getting something good out of them.

In more recent recordings spanning from the 1930s – 1970s, digitized tapes not only offered further contextual insights but also enabled us to engage dynamically. In the tapes we would listen to music that has already been crossed by the border, the ethnographers had genuine interest in music, and they operated within an ethical framework.

However, we encountered music that cannot be traced solely through a geographic designation, but music which has been blended in different territories, adapted in different settings, carrying in its rhythm an untraceable code – we would question the originality and purity which was pursued by the disciplinary regimes of scientific knowledge in earlier recordings, bringing to light a critical awareness of the history of recording technologies and their implication in processes of extraction.

To listen to the border in the archive is to listen to the flows and journeys that facilitate the encounter of musical worlds. We understood these events through a listening positionality, which provides us with a gateway to "re-socialize" music with people of the diaspora (sonic diaspora). As described in *Sonora*, my first approach to working with migrant musicians, it is the people of the diaspora that carry a similar condition to the untraceable code which music carries. Once that music reaches other territories and gets blended in the daily imagination of communities, a Sonic Diaspora is constituted.

A "critical listening positionality" (2020, p. 11) as xwélmexw scholar Dylan Robinson describes, encourages us to question how we can become more attuned to the filters of race, class, gender, and ability that shape our listening experiences. However, I would lean more towards what decolonial thinker Rolando Vázquez proposes when considering "a call for a positionality that involves listening, thinking, and feeling" (2020, p. 155) in relation to what is referred to as the "colonial difference" (Mignolo, 2002, p. 58) – those who have been marginalized and silenced by discourses centered on modernity, postmodernity, and Western civilization. By reading both Robinson and Vázquez I find a horizon where I can meet with musicians of many diasporas, through collectively listening to the materials of the archive and embodying their rhythmic histories. In doing so, we have attuned to a listening positionality, engaging with different bodily and geographical territories.

In the collaboration with the various musicians, our initial questions always centered on the personal significance of the music we engaged with. We would share how the recordings either forged a space of connection between us or induced tension. We would discuss our perception of "traditional music" within the canon and challenging notions of temporality. We queried the role of categories by asking what belongs to the traditional, and how we delineate contemporary or new music. How can we name the feeling arising from music? How to account for the feeling that is beyond the grasp of spoken language but communicated through rhythm and movement? This aspect became a focal point of our exchange.

Defining a rhythm as "out of tempo" or out of tune allowed us to question the positionality from which we enunciate such definitions. This became a challenge when listening to the mountain music of Peru. We heard a young woman singing with varying tones, oscillating in and out of rhythm. In its rootedness, we perceived how these women echoed each other, following the chants of birds, banging their drums, traversing the aural territory that surrounded them. The standard interpretations of music, which categorize in metric systems and temporal constraints, produced uncomfortable feelings. We frequently wanted to detach ourselves from the need to define, categorize, and measure with mathematical precision, we would rather exist in each other's embodiment of music.

We embraced error and imprecision as a mode of playing music, we often referred to these tensions and intellectual clashes as "oleajes" ("waves"). They became alive during improvisation. When identifying music through "oleajes," we recognized a deterritorialization of rhythm, prompting reflections on the meanings of belonging and origin. In this sense, listening to the "oleajes," or waves of time, uncategorized us from the limitations of western music and its colonial structures.

In the Caribbean, the interplay of violence, colonization, displacement, and labor exploitation has left an indelible mark on the evolution of musical expression and music technology. When we immerse ourselves in the resonance of Tassa drums – a traditional cyclindrical drum performed during weddings and celebrations – we are tapping into one of the many Indian music styles originating from the Bhojpuri region of Northern India.

Between 1845 and 1917, following the abolition of slavery and the subsequent scarcity of free labor for sugar production, indentureship programs emerged importing men and women to various regions, including the Americas and Fiji, as a source of cheap labor. While immigrants arrived from China, Portugal, and Africa, the largest contingent hailed from India. Known as *Jahaji*, or shipmen, they brought with them a wealth of knowledge encompassing instruments, rhythms, religious and musical practices, shaping the diasporic Indian communities that persist today – particularly in various parts of the United States and the Caribbean Basin.

When delving into recordings of Trinidad and Tobago, it becomes imperative to recognize the historical violence that transported the sounds of Tassa drumming across the Atlantic. However, acknowledging its conditionality of travel opens up narratives of resilience. Artistic form resists monoculture, eradication and extraction. This realization prompts us to emphasize the conditions that bear witness to a forceful memory, a transborder remembrance, evolving, and sustaining itself within communities of the diaspora.

The richness found in Tassa drumming transcends the implicit history of violence; it lies in the communities that carried these rhythms. We listen to the border in their music. The Tassa drum imparts a profound source of knowledge: history is far more intricate than linear narratives of "us and them." The sounds of the Tassa drums stand as unwavering witnesses to complex histories across the Atlantic.

While this doesn't absolve the violence that has marred history, it beckons us to engage in a more profound listening – attuning ourselves to the narratives conveyed by those who engage with the materiality of musical instruments, the rhythmicity of songs and the oral journeys shared by those who hold them.

The recordings of Trinidad and Tobago also contained contextual explanations of the functions of different drums within the different songs. Musicians would elaborate on the purpose of their unique rhythms, and even share personal experiences related to the vibrant music scene. Listening to these processes transcends the mere quest for understanding origins and questions of belonging; collective engagement with musical journeys offers a portal to the diverse temporalities that European languages cannot encapsulate or define with spoken or written word. Rhythm precedes us; it sustains our bodily memories and senses through playfulness and the practice of improvisation.

During a period of February to August of 2022, our exchange with musicians continued, we reflected on how musical gestures encapsulated a repository of knowledge. I refer to the communities with whom I work as a Sonic Diaspora. This community is characterized by the musical memory, oral traditions, and listening practices they carry from places of encounter to further geographic locations and cultural contexts, dislocating nationhood from the knowledge inscribed in sonic territories. A Sonic Diaspora is able to inhabit any geography in a transborder condition, challenging the fixed notions of citizenship and culture; it is a community that is constituted through processes such as migration, colonization, globalization, and technological advancements. The Sonic Diaspora transfers memory and knowledge through performing musical memory and exchanging with others. In our conviviality, musical improvisation serves as the horizon where we reflect on the complexity of human mobility, when improvising with the Sonic Diaspora, a portal unfolds, guiding us along an unpredictable path.

We navigate this path, by attuning to the echoes of journeys across seas. The closest description to the profound feeling it evokes can be similar to imagining the image of exchanging waters, a river transforming into an ocean, an oceanic energy manifesting through a sequence of waves clashing.

In an attempt to name the temporality describing such exchanges between musical worlds, I refer to "Tiempo Ritmo," to an unmeasurable time, a time that exists, yet it cannot be framed within a metric system, it is a time in silence that expands through the body. It comes in motion as we breathe it, embodying the fluidity of the coming and going of water. In my conversations with the Sonic Diaspora, we reflect on the crossroads of rhythm and the points of encounter which have catapulted musical worlds.

MUSICA PARA TERCER PAISAJE (MUSIC FOR A THIRD LANDSCAPE)

In my film *Musica para Tercer Paisaje*,[4] I filmed musician Laura Robles playing a percussive lead through the sound of a saxophone and a double bass. As the performance unfolds, we can listen to an elegant gallop of a horse through the Peruvian cajón. When I showcased this film in Kinshasa, Congo, during my presentation *La Frontière comme pratique: Sentir / Penser' la frontière*,[5] a woman approached me at the end of my presentation, revealing that the rhythms Laura played resonated with those from her village on the outskirts of Kinshasa. She shared how these rhythms travelled to diverse territories and were played by her ancestors for different celebrations, handed down through generations and taught by her mentors.

When I returned to Berlin, I eagerly recounted this revelation to Laura, emphasizing that the music she played in the film originated from the outskirts of Kinshasa. Together, we imagined and speculated on the moment when that rhythm might have travelled directly to the coast of Peru. We envisioned the possibility that the rhythm had either made the journey or evolved into a sonic syncretism, as a blending of diverse musical rhythms, local histories, affinities and senses that created a new sonic experience. Nevertheless, it carried a code that could only be cracked through improvisation with Huguette Tolinga, the woman who approached me at the end of my presentation and someone who has since become a dear friend and collaborator.

In the subsequent year, I produced *Rhythm and Memory*,[6] a performative presentation where I invite Laura Robles and Huguette Tolinga to immerse themselves in shared musical exploration. Through a one hour and thirty-minute nonstop improvisational session, Huguette and Laura brought these memories to life. In this rhythmic experience, they rendered the originality and purity of rhythms irrelevant, highlighting how rhythm is a language sustained through the body. The language of rhythm achieves a level of attunement that connects us with what I call a *Tiempo Ritmo*. In this experience, I realized that *Tiempo Ritmo* is about that moment in time when music crosses territories, the point of departure of a rhythm towards another geography, a deterritorialization of knowledge and a constitution of a new one. My profound interest in working with the Sonic Diaspora comes from this intricate process – the one revelation that music enables through improvisation and embodied listening, the "moment of crossing."

OLEAJES (WAVES)

The Berlin Phonogramm-Archiv, like any other ethnographic collection, categorizes music by national regions or territories. However, we have found deeper meaning by weaving the materials through the imagination of *Oleajes, Waves* which echo rhythmic and harmonic lineages from different geographies. When we listen to music, we acknowledge how colonization, extraction and displacement processes are present in the coming together of musical worlds. It is not a coincidence that we can sense the presence of the Indian Tassa drums arriving on the shores of the Caribbean. In other worlds of meaning, when we listen to Asian winds in the Andes mountains, we contemplate the sonic encounters forged through the vast expanse of the Pacific Ocean. We sense the resonance of bamboo flutes reverberating through the southern mountains of the cordillera, connected to the passage of oriental trade routes through *Abya Yala*. The synchronicity in Andean procession music and its resonant mirror with the first nation people of the north. Why do the ritual rhythms of Angola and Senegal align so closely with the Carnival festivities in Brazil? The Atlantic Ocean bears witness to the atrocities of slave trade and the silent resistance of bodies across continents. Memory lives in its changing waters; therefore, we choose to work with its flows. Many sound recordings of ethnographic collections are intertwined in such violent processes. It is essential to discern which recordings follow established protocols and which ones signify encounters that offer glimpses into the possibilities of these musical meetings.

We approached the archive of the Berlin Phonogramm-Archiv by thinking with the Sonic Diaspora. What sustains the harmonies, acoustics, and rhythms we resemble so often? How can we put these rhythms back into circulation through our bodies? Improvising with the Sonic Diaspora allowed us to listen to each other and embody the very essence of our conversations. Our focus was to listen to the border, to music that has already been in contact with plural sonic worlds.

I reflect on the possibility of musical restitution, not necessarily by giving it back to the community of origin, but by playing music back into circulation, performing the archive and expanding it from the rhythmless cages of museums, outside of the ethnographic experience, into the body and out into public space, shared with the Sonic Diaspora. Re-embodied back through musical improvisation. *Cosmoaudiciones* aims to find new meanings in sound recordings, to re-dignify the extracted voices, to improvise with the recordings as a way to address the absences of histories.

TIEMPO RITMO

The sum of thoughts gathered during our engagement with the Berlin Phonogramm-Archiv manifested in a series of performances and musical lectures which narrate the journey of rhythm. Different works came alive during our listening period, acknowledging time outside of western metrics. In our musical improvisation, we can listen to the journeys of resistance and re-existence struggles through the musical worlds that travel in and out of the Atlantic into the Americas. We have improvised alongside many recordings found in the archive. We have hosted each other in rhythm. We recognize, through music improvisation, the legacies that have brought worlds of meaning into and out of the Atlantic.

Tiempo Ritmo is a time that exists in the gravity of ocean crossings, *oleajes* that come alive through the totality of winds above the seas. It is a time that takes form as an open cycle. It comes into deep consciousness along the aural movement of blending waters. It is the coming and going that finds rest among the calm of coastlines. It is a time that lives through other waters that exceed territorial delimitation. This is not a singular time. It is a temporality that expands into rhythmicity, performing its boundless travel into the breathing of earthly bodies.

NOTES

1. Due to the Covid-19 pandemic, in Germany, on March 13, 2020, stores, restaurants, bars, and discos had to close in order to prevent the spreading of the disease. In Berlin, any type of gathering in public places was not allowed, and more than two people were not allowed to meet, with the exception of families, households, or partners. For more about Covid-19 in Berlin, please see: https://www.fu-berlin.de/en/sites/coronavirus/index.html

2. *Sonora* is part of a broader project by artistic endeavor *Owned by Others* which seeks to make interventions into the narratives and public spaces of Berlin. This particular project, running from 2020 – 21, brought together a series of artists in order to examine Museum Island and its geographies in critical dialogue with their own localities worldwide. The artist commissions involved interventions in public space, performances, and walks. For video documentation of *Sonora*, please see my website https://miguelbuenrostro.net/Sonora-constellations-copy (accessed: 13 February 2024). For more about *Owned by Others*, please see https://ownedbyothers.org/ (accessed 13 February 2024).

3. *Cosmoaudiciones* is an artistic project by Migeul Buenrostro funded by the Berlin Senat, curated by Brandon LaBelle and with the participation of Laura Robles, Trigo Santana, Fabiano Lima, Robby Geerken, Tom Kessler, Banda Hodi, and the Orquesta Experimental de Instrumentos Nativo, Eli Wewentxu, Huguette Tolinga. See further details on my website https://cosmoaudiciones.org/PROJECT-Cosmoaudiciones (accessed 13 February 2024).

4. *Música para tercer paisaje*, (2020) Link: https://vimeo.com/597647740, 15" Film, Performance, 3 Channel, Installation

5.	*La Fronrtière comme pratique: Sentir / Penser' la frontière* was an artistic presentation by Miguel Buenrostro during the exhibition Kinzonzi curated by Lydia Schellhammer and Christ Mukenge, in Kinshasa Congo. The presentation hosted dialogues on the border as place of thinking but also as a place of artistic production. See further details on my website https://labkontempo.com/fr/salle-dexposition-2021/ (accessed 11 April 2024).

6.	*Rhythm and Memory* was an artistic project by Miguel Buenrostro that brought together percussionists Laura Robles and Huguette Tolinga in a dynamic collaboration. the performance explored themes of liberation, migration, and interconnectedness through music. The event was held during the Miziki Program curated by Miguel Buenrostro, Lydia Schellhammer and Christ Mukenge; as part of the Berlin Edition of Kinzonzi exhibition. See further details on the website https://pantopia-music.org/en/album-rhythm-memory/(accessed 11 April 2024).

BIBLIOGRAPHY

Anzaldúa, Gloria. (1987) *Borderlands La Frontera, The New Mestiza*. San Francisco: Aunt Lute books.

Galeano, Eduardo. (2011) *Los Hijos de los días*, Uruguay; Editorial Siglo XXI.

Koch, Lars-Christian, Albrecht Wiedmann and Susanne Ziegle, 'The Berlin Phonogramm-Archiv: A treasury of sound recordings', (2004), p 228.

Lenkersdorf, Carlos. (2011) *Aprender a escuchar, Enseñanzas Maya-Tojolabales*, México D.F.: Plaza Valdéz Editores.

Mignolo, Walter. (2011) "The Geopolitics Of Sensing and Knowing: on (de)coloniality, border thinking and epistemic disobedience," *Postcolonial Studies*, Vol. 14, No. 3, pp. 273 – 283. 101 (1): 57 – 96.

Mignolo, Walter. (2002) "The Geopolitics Of Knowledge and the Colonial Difference," South Atlantic Quarterly 101 (1): 57 – 96.

Vázquez, Rolando. (2020) *Vistas of Modernity, Decolonial aesthesis and the end of the contemporary*. Amsterdam: Jap Sam Books.

REBECCA COLLINS

Detectives of the Invisible: Towards a Cosmological Listening Practice OR HOW TO HEAR ELUSIVE PARTICLES

I. A SCIENTIFIC SÉANCE?

In an email I send to composer Adam Matschulat to initiate our collaboration on "Energies not Forms not Figures" (Collins and Matschulat, 2023) I state how I want the work to feel as though "this could be a seance, but it never quite is." We are working on a twenty-minute sound art piece related to my crossdisciplinary research project *Parameters for Understanding Uncertainty* (P4UU) and have been exchanging materials.[1] I send Adam extracts of performance writing, field recordings, and interview extracts. To conduct the research, which focuses on how artistic research methodologies meet those used in the physical sciences, I spent fifteen months in residence at the Institute for Theoretical Physics, located on the campus of the Autonomous University in Madrid. Throughout my residency I listened in and posed impossible listening-related questions to physicists attempting to unravel what occurred in the first few minutes of the universe.

In this essay I share examples of creative practice I assembled when writing the text score for "Energies not Forms not Figures" (Collins and Matschulat, 2023). These served as thinking companions throughout my stay at the Institute for Theoretical Physics. The examples include a range of practices; from pictorial depictions of invisible energies, to text-based practices which listen in to inner voices, to an experimental novel that considers how planetary and interpersonal energies might intersect yet, above all, be listened to. I want to seriously consider the potential of extra sensorial perception and its documents. I intersperse extracts of the text score from "Energies not Forms not Figures," which featured in the exhibition *Listening to Dark Matter* (2023) with these findings.[2] By juxtaposing these texts, I bring together an unlikely assemblage of "data" that attunes to otherwise energies to consider how, as Sophia K. Rosa queries in her book *Radical Intimacy*, "liberation [might] [...] be possible" (2023, p. 72) from disciplinary binds evidencing how we are "always capable of being otherwise" (ibid.).

At the Institute for Theoretical Physics in Madrid I become very interested in ongoing unknowns related to our planet and its position within the universe. I discover a large percentage of invisible matter, surrounding our everyday existence, is yet to be fully understood. Known as dark matter, despite arguments that the term "transparent" is a better fit, I quickly become fascinated by the idea of an elusive, missing mass holding galaxies (including ours) together. Whilst, what are known as planned detection experiments aim to reveal further details of this mysterious substance, its particle nature is unknown.[3] Gravitational evidence from early astrophysical and cosmological optical observations, found in the work of Vera Rubin and her team in the 1970s, proves there is an unexplained phenomenon in the form of an unseen mass which inhibits stars from flying off into the galaxy. As physicist Lisa Randall notes "billions of dark matter particles pass through each of us every second. Yet no one notices [...] they are there. The effect of even billions of dark matter particles on us is miniscule" (2015, p. 20). At once a conundrum for new physics and a totally mundane proposition as our everyday lives unfold completely ignorant of this imperceptible milieu.

A number of international collaborations are currently invested in direct detection efforts to better understand the particle nature of dark matter.[4] Within this context I am intrigued to discover several experiments are turning to the sonic. I have based my research stay in Spain for this reason. As part of my project, I undertake two field visits to research groups whose approach to dark matter detection makes use of sound or listening in some way. The first is to the Canfranc Underground Laboratory where, deep underneath Mount Tobazo in the Pyrenees Mountains, cosmic silence is cultivated to reduce noisy interference from cosmic rays and other sources of terrestrial background signal. The second is to the Laboratory of Acoustics for the Detection of Astroparticles at the Polytechnical University in Gandía who use hydrophones, deep below the surface of the Mediterranean Sea, to listen in on collisions between high energy particles.[5] Science historian Cyrus C. M. Mody writing about the role of listening in relation to the work of science laboratories is adamant that "listening, hearing, attuning, and other ear-work are integral to much that goes on" (2005, p. 176). Mody also makes a claim that sound is bound up in the embodied knowledge produced in laboratory settings and calls for thicker descriptions to make more of how sound is used by science in order to gain insight into "issues of situated and embodied knowledge" (2005, p. 193) within experimental settings. Indeed, whilst artistic residencies have increasingly turned their focus towards current advances in physics (see, for example Arts @ CERN) to date the majority of projects make use of data sonification to represent scientific research.[6] The lived and situated experience, connected to sonic-driven scientific experiments, as refracted through creative account-making remains undocumented.

Whilst we may never truly get a feel for the minute alterations within our surrounding environs, nothing prevents us from imagining how energy exchanges operate at imperceptible scales. I take inspiration from Fred Moten and Wu Tsang, who ask, "What if we reinitiate the problem of physics as a problem of feel?" (2016, p. 31) Equally, I'm invested in more affective approaches to invisible matter, building on what audio theorist Douglas Kahn has noted. Kahn states that it is much easier to empathize with living creatures that have eyes and limbs (sentience and technics), or with objects as these occupy fairly stable locations than with ever-moving nondescript energies (2013, p. 17). Surely some emancipatory potential can be harnessed by thinking and embodying approaches that linger alongside that which is at the limit of the perceivable? I consider how to practice and conduct listening in this way and how this might be a form of response-ability, that Donna Haraway advocates for (2016). Equally, I find affiliation in the work of Jane Bennett on "The Sonorous Cosmos" (2001, p. 166) and "Ethical Energetics" (ibid., p. 131) where the latter, as noted by Brandon LaBelle in *Sonic Agency* (2018), pushes for a form of listening as agency. Bennett notes how, through listening, we can access the ever-changing relations around us. Bennett encourages we attune ourselves to an ethics of energetics as she states "Through sound, through the various refrains we invent, repeat, and catch from nonhumans, we receive news of the cosmic energies to which we humans are always in close, molecular proximity" (2001, p. 168). If we reorientate ourselves toward the multiple energies in circulation and proximity to our own, perhaps we can rework the current energy paradigm. Political scientist Cara New Daggett queries the endless human desire for energy claiming that "A genealogy of energy suggests that there are other ways of knowing and living energy, and that energy and work can be decoupled" (2019, p. 11). I think of these positions as potential grounds for a cosmological listening practice.

I begin to consider, during my research residency at the Institute for Theoretical Physics, if it is possible to train our senses to perceive elusive particles. I pursue this query over several months in a variety of formats. I listen *in* to qualitative talks on the history of dark matter; I lend an ear to conversations at dark matter conferences; I read popular science texts; I set up a four-part interdisciplinary seminar series; I curate a workshop for artists and scientists in the rural Basque country; I watch YouTube videos created by investigators at the Institute: I attune to the post-seminar gossip: I hang out at weekly coffee meet ups and in the corridors of the building. I read outreach posters aloud into my recording device. I dialogue with my host for the project, dark matter investigator, Dr David Cerdeño. At some point, Cerdeño and I formulate the question "Can we listen to dark matter?" In doing so, we forge a tentative link between technological apparatus used in dark matter detection techniques, figuring such setups as sensorial extensions able to complement our habitual perceptive capabilities.[7] We use this proposition to structure a series of collaborative talks at science museums and high energy physics training schools.[8] We are finding crossovers between sound/listening studies and physics. In March 2023 I use this provocation to structure my exhibition *Listening to Dark Matter* (2023) where sound art, also very much an invisible medium, is the protagonist.[9]

I situate this project within planetary studies whereby the terrestrial, and the disciplinary are reconsidered. I'm drawn to a planetary framework to embrace uncertainty and relationality thereby disturbing hierarchical distinctions and pre-supposed subjects e.g., humanity, the West, etc. By collating this minor composition of practices I'm invested in unearthing creative articulations that redirect energies (human and nonhuman) to, in turn, redirect our collective imagination. I'm drawn to the planetary and the planet, as Gayatri Chakravorty Spivak notes, the planet is situated "in the species of alterity, belonging to another system" (2003, p. 73) one I believe to be open to intuitive and cross-disciplinary thinking outside the logics of capitalism. Or, as human geographer Oli Mould notes, "planetary thinking contains within it praxes that can more readily critique – and mobilize action against [...] hegemonic and colonial thinking" (2023, p. 2). I write this text against a backdrop of unprecedented and multiple humanitarian and displacement crises in what feels like a timely and opportune moment to reconsider the underside of science.

> Energies, not forms, not figures (chant)
> Cosmic proportions abound
> Stay to sift and sieve molecules til morning
> Not a molecule, no
> An atom
> An invisible atomic component

A neutrino

Dark matter?

It's seasonal some will say

A laugh secludes security

Ideas illuminate points on a line

Concerns quiver

Dust free for now

II.   VIBRATORY POTENTIAL

A faded A4 color printout of *Mater [Materia]* (1912) by Italian futurist, Umberto Boccioni sits alone in a pale grey acid-free archive box (No.4 of 4) from *Parameters for Understanding Uncertainty*. For over a year the printout of *Mater* is blue-tacked to the wall of B14, the office I occupy on the ground floor of the Theoretical Physics Institute. An integral aspect of my approach to the research project is to inhabit and make use of this office on a daily basis. From B14 I attune and aurally attend to the nuances of the scholars, administrators, and senior managers researching contemporary conundrums at the forefront of new physics. Their everyday rhythms, frustrations, and successes score the background of my time in the building. I imagine the printout twitching as I write, my attention attuning to the images' details now imprinted on my mind's eye. The central figure, Boccioni's Mother, is surrounded by shards and fragments all containing smaller images. Voluminous yet untethered; a red ghost-like horse moves across the right knee of the central figure (strangely portentous given the circumstances of the artists death in a riding accident). A red ghost-like man walks across the left-hand side in the opposite direction. Part of a house sits on the top right-hand side with two doors. This is an image in motion, a vibratory picture filled with orange, red, green and blue tones. Memories, turbulences, and traumas orbit the mother figure who sits in the middle visibly perturbed by the swirling forces. The work feels like a pictorial reminder of how, as Randall notes "ordinary matter – such as that contained in stars, gas and people –

constitutes only 15 per cent" (2015, p. 13) and yet, such phenomena greatly influence our feelings – the recognizable figures and forms that constitute a life dance and haunt the central figure.

Immaterial memories are rendered material through the medium of paint. A kind of transduction which hints at the idea that all life experience is imprinted either onto your body or onto the atmosphere you occupy. For art historian Linda Dalrymple Henderson, Boccioni's *Mater* is considered, alongside Francisek Kupka's *Amorpha, Fugue in Two Colors* (1912), as exemplifying *vibratory modernism* (2013). This, broadly speaking, describes how emergent discoveries within science and technology of the nineteenth and twentieth century, such as electromagnetism and thermodynamics, were depicted in art and science. What links these two paintings, according to Henderson, is a shared concern for pictorially depicting the ether. From the early 1900s up until about 1930 the ether (also spelt as aether) was an unknown substance that filled all space. It was generally thought of, as science historian Bruce Hunt notes, a "thin elastic solid or 'jelly' stretching across interstellar space" (2002, p. 100). Many physicists of the time were optimistic it would, as Hunt indicates, "link together everything in the Universe" (ibid., p. 99). The electromagnetic field, closely related to the ether, became the successor to the majority of its functions. Eventually the ether was scientifically disproved as a fictional construction. That said, the idea of invisible energies coursing through individuals, sites, and situations still lends itself to the artistic imagination. Boccioni considered the futurist painter a clairvoyant of sorts, one able to connect with invisible vibrating forces. This is the technique he applies to the portrait of his mother evidencing, through painterly techniques, the ethereal formations in circulation around an individual.

The idea that memories of moments lived can reverberate beyond our individual experience of them and be untethered to strict chronological time is explored extensively in Virginia Woolf's *Moments of Being*. In these posthumously published autobiographical writings Woolf questions whether "things we have felt with great intensity have an existence independent of our minds" (1978, p. 78). Taking this further still, she ponders whether these things are "still in existence?" (ibid.) Woolf gestures to the idea that certain sensuous experiences endure, often accruing significance and mixing with moments from other times. A stretchy membrane of sorts accessible through memory. In "A Sketch of the Past," the first essay in the volume, Woolf gives an account of her early years, predominantly spent at St Ives in Cornwall, through a sequence of impressions. If she had been a painter, she postulates, she would have made "a picture of curved petals, of shells, of things that were semi-transparent" (ibid., p. 76). She desires the creation of "large and dim" (ibid., p. 76) versions of these items, without clear outlines. Woolf also wished to include sound in these images claiming "sound and sight seem to make equal parts of these first impressions" (ibid., p. 76). She cites the cawing of rooks, the sound of waves breaking, and the splash of a wave drawing in again. These sonorous traces, taken from her infancy and childhood, are so vividly described it is as though they caress her as she writes.

Stretchy gelatinous descriptions of childhood replay as aural effects as though plucked from the ether. Sound, and the quality of audition, receives specific attention as she describes how "the quality of air above Talland House seemed to suspend sound, to let it sink down slowly, as if it were caught in a blue gummy veil" and earlier, when qualifying the sound of the rooks' caw, she describes how "sound seems to fall through an elastic, gummy air; which holds it up; which prevents it from being sharp and distinct." A penetrable stretchy membrane of sorts. Woolf's attention to sound and listening is a constant and occurs throughout the writing. This includes reference to hearing voices, her mothers in particular. At one point she speculates whether there might, in the future, be a technology that enables you to fit a plug to the wall "and listen in to the past" convinced that "strong emotion must leave its trace" (ibid., p. 78). She is quite convinced of these traces being available as the main question she poses is not whether they exist but how to re-attach ourselves so we can "live our lives through from the start" (ibid.).

Her nonsensical stuff invades your everyday, swirling all around, a constant hum that won't go away, indeed, in existence from our very first days, our very first hours, our very first minutes, our very first seconds,

indeed, indeed, indeed long before they were even called HOURS. MIN-
UTES. SECONDS. Y3AH. an ongoing drone of discontENT FAlling over
and over and over again on deaf ears. AND GUESS WHAT there are
still trillions and trillions and trillions of her zipping through your *little*
nose right now. AND in the middle of the night barely audible articulations erupt in peaks and troughs, *quote* she is seasonal *unquote*, a position impossible to re-approve. DON'T WORRY. Only weakly interact-
ing. Y3AH. Low energy remnants. OKAY. Soft presence. Y3AH. Dedicate,
dedicate, dedicate, decades in international collective attempts. NOTE:
She eludes the exact pinpointing of a place. Remember parameters help
by precisely gesturing to where she is NOT, finding out more nothings
will lead to somethings, *quote* nothing will come of nothing *unquote*.

[field recording Canfranc Underground Laboratory]

III.   WRITING / READING TO DISPLACE / DISRUPT

In the early 1970s performance artist and poet Hannah Weiner, a member
of the Language poetry movement, began to receive a form of dictation she
termed clairvoyance.[10] Her writing practice operated as testimony to this act.
She claimed she began to see and receive words as though etched "on my fore-
head IN THE AIR on other people on the typewriter on the page" (2014, p. 7).
The use of capitals or italics indicates the words as they appeared to Weiner.[11]
The book is full of everyday, mundane experiences from her personal life yet
also reads, to some extent, as a catalogue for the countercultural movements of
the era. Her social interactions with well-known artists on the scene at the time
such as Phil Niblock, Bernadette Mayer, Steve Reich, John Cage and Charles
Bernstein (amongst others) feature heavily. In a film on Public Access Poetry TV
Weiner reads the work aloud with Sharon Mattlin and Peggy De Coursey indi-
cating the intended choral tri-vocal style of the writing.[12] Her overarching experience of clairvoyance was such that it caused her to state, "words see us" and
"we are spoken by language" (Ibid., p. 129).

63

Weiner's clairvoyance can be considered, as literary critic Judith Goldman notes, as a "technique for estranging the normalcy that mystifies us" (2001, p. 122) causing us to question the extent to which language arrives to us and is given voice. For Alan Ramón Clinton, in line with Weiner's earlier clairvoyant works *The Fast* (1992) and *Weeks* (1990), her practice operates as a form of capitalist critique toward how certain subjects are produced and conditioned by the system their lives unfold within (2012). This is acutely clear in the passage where she tries to resist buying a pair of pants whilst, simultaneously, the Apollo-13 rocket launch is taking place.

> DOWN at the door so OK I go see these maroon velvet pants
> I'm not BUY $40
> pants BLOOMINGDALES all over again I leave GO TO
> COUNTDOWN: refuge,
> get in a taxi, start for home, no peace, get out GO TO
> COUNTDOWN ok it's only
> money go back and buy the pants it's better than seeing GO TO
> COUNTDOWN
> for the rest of my life peace so they fit well.

Weiner offers, via the multi-vocal approach and textual interjections on the page, a form of disruption to the reader, perhaps what can even be described as a radical disruption, to the act of reading and what it means to be *read*. Weiner states:

> When I see words I am also able to know, by reading or handling a book, as example, if an author is a friend, what her illness is, what books she prefers whether she knows what to do for herself, whether to read her at all. ... clairvoyantly I am the other to myself ... In my nonclairvoyant work there is no person. (Weiner, 1991)

One of Weiner's main claims here, as noted by liberal arts scholar Patrick Durgin, is to position subjectivity not as "an entity but [as] a dynamic" (Durgin, (2004)

p. 4 citing Lyn Hejinian (2000) *Language of Inquiry*, p. 203). This position was shared and actively explored at the "Symposium on the Person," part of which was subsequently published in *Poetics Journal* (issue 9, 1991) whereby the figure of "the person" was discussed as distinct from the "self as self-same entity" (ibid). In Weiner's work, experience is separated from notions of individual intention. The "person" is considered another element in the world, one who is also subject to the indeterminacies of that world, or as I might add, the planet. To return to Oli Mould's discussion of the planetary, as referenced in the introduction, "planetary thinking [...] recognises our material and psychological intimacy with the living atmo / bio / eco-sphere around us" (2023, p. 6). Whilst worthy of a longer discussion, ultimately Weiner's approach to writing as a form of documentation for her non-intentional indeterminate encounters with words seeks to displace the subject, sense-making, and how knowledge operates.

For the purposes of this essay, by debunking the notion of the subject, and through closer alignment with the nonhuman and the planetary, I want to suggest it is possible to get closer to thinking *otherwise* about how / who we are in the world and the relations and hierarchies that structure our interactions. Social scientist Akwugo Emejulu in *Fugitive Feminism* (2022) queries the usefulness of human as category. Emejulu is predominantly building on the work of Sylvia Wynter and Katherine McKittrick (2015) who question "what it means to be human and, more important, how we might give humanness a different future" (2015, p. 10). Throughout her book Emejulu adopts a bricolage approach interweaving the legacies of thinking by Black studies scholars with autobiographical detail. In doing so she lingers on what it might mean to not belong to the category of the human and, ultimately what it might mean to be free. She cites Combahee River Collective, who state, "If Black women were free, it would mean that everyone else would have to be free since our freedom would necessitate the destruction of all systems of oppression" (1983, pp. 264 – 74 cited in Emejulu, 2022, p. 23). Emejulu relinquishes desire to identify with the category of human given the depth of corruption and hierarchical structures such a naming implies. Ultimately pointing to how the invention of category and the invention of race is ontologically vacuous.

For Denise Ferreira da Silva, writing in relation to Moten and Tsang's physics-related performance project *Gravitational Feel* in the accompanying publication *Who Touched Me?* asks:

> Why not assume that beyond their physical (bodily and geographic) conditions of existence, in their fundamental constitution, at the sub-atomic level, humans exist entangled with everything (animate and inanimate) else in the universe (2016, p. 43).

Indeed, the notion of "*separability*" (italics in original, ibid., 43), a term that Ferreira da Silva goes on to analyze becomes, as she states, problematic, in terms of being a "privileged ontological principle" (ibid.). If we think beyond separating humans from nonhumans, the actions, habits, products and processes attached from what we have come to associate with the human then we really begin to disrupt and question ethical practices. This, of course also requires a shift in knowing and thinking, a move beyond determinacy in the Cartesian sense where the mind holds the power of determination or knowing as a kind of "efficient causality" (ibid.).

> Speak this text aloud AND only in the absence of dust AND ideally in cosmic silence.

> A LANGUAGE gathers in the depths, under water, under mountains, under ice. Grab a pen, a notepad, set up artificial intelligence systems. Saying "A LANGUAGE" is a bold place to start. Strip out the I's. Ask if we possess notation techniques for the unknown. Strip out the O's. Maybe first check what is meant by possess. Strip out the U's. Verify what is meant by UNKNOWN. Wind up watches THEN note the passing of seconds, minutes, hours, months, years. PAUSE. Consider this a collective task. Use LEDs to indicate oxygen levels, CB radios in all vehicles, a hub, control entry and exit. A TIMELY REMINDER: the arrival of the ELUSIVE will not be announced. Ask if we possess the ability to detect. Ask if we

are READY. NOTE: a map, when on the wall, indicates clearly where you are, not where you aren't. Ask if we are STEADY. CONSIDER: What parameters are necessary for something to occur the same way twice? REALISE: If you are uncertain, it is better to surround yourself with even less certainty. WRITE: STAY AWAY from the SURE ZONE on your wrist and above all, beware your epistemic desire.

IV. EPISTEMIC WEARINESS / WARINESS

Radical British experimental writer, Christine Brooke-Rose, following her four orthodox novels began to experiment with readers' expectations from 1964 onwards. Brooke-Rose had particular interests in Heisenberg's quantum physics which ultimately altered her narrative style.[13] This is most evident in *Such* a novel that is not indeterminate in its form yet is about indeterminacy. The novel operates by presenting a reflection on what the act of interpretation does thereby making the reader question how knowledge is implicated in the world around us. To the extent that, in reading Brooke-Rose, we may become wary of our epistemic desires and, indeed, all acts of interpretation.

In *Such* indeterminacy and the role of the interpreter comes as a warning to knowing too much. Too much knowledge can be dangerous to meaning and might best be left as undifferentiated potential. Writing in 1965 Brooke-Rose states "it has become a truism that, in sub microscopic terms, the object is affected by the instrument observing it – part of the famous principle of uncertainty which has indirectly affected all our philosophy and all our attitudes" (1965, p. 93). Within the text of *Such* this becomes even more evident:

A principle of indeterminacy applies, compared, I mean, with the determinacy in regard to large numbers of atoms. The moment you try to find out its condition the very process of investigation must disturb it. So with ideas and people, compared to mass ideas, mass people. And causes (2007, p. 363).

One of the central characters of the novel is Larry, who "collects silences" (ibid., p. 203). Larry goes through a number of epistemological challenges. The particular twist Brooke-Rose brings is to apply indeterminacy to people. As readers, we follow Larry through a variety of dream states, hallucinations and moments where planets and the orbits of people overlap. Larry goes through medical procedures and other encounters with potential future partners and offspring. Toward the end of the novel, Larry, in dialogue with another character, Elizabeth further evidences the interest of Brooke-Rose in the Heisenberg Uncertainty Principle.

> — Larry, everyone deserves the attention of definitiveness.
> — Even if they prefer the uncertainty principle?
> — They only pretend to prefer it. While they have to. You used to say that. Someone would come along and find a unified theory that would do away with indeterminate interpretations, you'd say and revert to causality. I thought perhaps you might.
> — I thought so too. In psychic terms at least. But I didn't. In the meantime we do the best we can, some of us preferring to pretend causality exists, and others, others preferring to prefer its absence. But you can never know with absolute certainty that what look like the same particle, with the same identity —
> — Yes but for the practical purposes you have to, Larry, in the chemistry of people. Otherwise how can you live?
> — You can't. Not really. You pretend that you do. To save the appearances.
> — Larry, you can't honestly believe that.
>
> (*Such*, p. 387)

In a radio interview, given in late 1965, just after the publication of *Such*, Brooke-Rose was asked to comment on her use of the Uncertainty Principle within her writing, and the interest of French novelists in the "modern world of science" she states:

The modern scientific concept [is] that any object is affected by the instrument observing it. You can't actually see an electron jumping from one orbit to another, if indeed it jumps, and … the photon that you've got to use is going to affect its behaviour. And I think this is very important in the observation of reality; the moment you start observing it, it shifts. And I think this is a problem modern novelists have to face, that you can't just make a photograph of the reality immediately around you because it has already shifted by the very process of photographing it, and looking at it.

The perspective of astrophysics enables Brooke-Rose to combine two scales, namely the planetary and the microscopic. Human behaviors are considered in terms of shifting between being "waves and undulations" (2018, p. 273) to the ability of exchanging one's atoms with someone else's. Emotional states are announced such as one character, Stance's wife who "bombards the spare room with particles of a vague discontent" (Jordan (2018) p. 273 citing *Such*, p. 282) or, another character, Elizabeth who brings "particles of her self-absorption" (Jordan (2018) p. 273 citing *Such*, p. 379). Crucial to the novel is the conception of energy that operates "both as emotional and thermodynamic" as human energy is considered in terms of a resource that can waste itself, that which should be organized, and above-all listened to (see Brooke-Rose, 234).

Finally, in "Dynamic Gradients" in *London Magazine* Brooke-Rose states:

We must evolve a new way of thinking and reject the old universalistic and absolute concepts, especially our habit of identification, just as the scientists have done. If we do not, we shall continue to produce more and more semantic blockages in our nervous systems, more breakdowns in communication, more mental disturbances, in fact we would not be equipped to survive the evolutionary process (Brooke-Rose, 1965, pp. 89 – 96 cited in Joseph Darlington, 2017, p. 154).

The cultivation of a cosmological listening practice, one that is sensitive to shifts in the atmos / bios / eco-sphere or otherwise attuned to the planetary, the intuitive and the emotional "ethers," over the global and globalized capitalistic approaches can potentially do ourselves and our planet a favor. The promise, or premise of an invisible, transparent particle known to exist but as yet able to defy capture offers the tantalizing prospect of questioning our current orders of knowledge. My parting intention, through this exposition of creative thinking companions aims to consider what / how future discoveries might liberate us from old ways of thinking, disciplinary binds and imposed categories.

NOTES

1. *Parameters for Understanding Uncertainty: Creative Practice and Sonic Detection as Strategies for Scientific Outreach (P4UU)* was funded by a Royal Society of Edinburgh Early Career Saltire Fellowship, grant ID.1897 (2022 – 2023. See project website for further details https://projects.ift.uam-csic.es/p4uu/ (Accessed: 09 August 2023).

2. To listen to an extract from 'Energies not Forms not Figures' (Collins and Matschulat, 2023) see: https://on.soundcloud.com/Cr1zR (Accessed: 29 August 2023).

3. There are a number of international collaborations invested in direct detection efforts to better understand the particle nature of dark matter. The premise for such experiments is that some dark matter can be intercepted on Earth as dark matter moves through the universe. Direct detection experiments make use of highly sensitive technologies and materials to increasingly extend their reach and capability in order to detect these weak and rare events.

4. As dark matter is yet to be discovered the history of dark matter detection is still being written.

5. I write about the field visits more extensively in "On Listening in to the Scientific Mundane: Parameters for Understanding Uncertainty & Political Indeterminacy" *Performance Research*, Vol. 28. 4 (March 2024).

6. For an example of data sonification connected to dark matter detection, see Núria Bonet (2016), 'Sonification of Dark Matter: Challenges and Opportunities' *Proceedings of the Sound and Music Computing Conference.* For a compelling and recent exception to this, see Ain Bailey's "Tone Poem" (2024) which makes use of the bleeps, pings, drones and other sounds found with the physics laboratory. See also "Adventures in C.A.S" https://on.soundcloud.com/ RNmue. These works were created during Bailey's Cavendish Arts Science Fellowship at The Cavendish Laboratory (Department of Physics), University of Cambridge (UK).

7. Direct detection experiments make use of highly sensitive technologies and materials to increasingly extend their reach and capability in order to detect these weak and rare events.

8. For documentation on research seminars, see project website *Parameters for Understanding Uncertainty (P4UU)* https://projects.ift.uam-csic.es/p4uu/elementor-2076/ (Accessed: 30 January 2024). Also, forthcoming article Rebecca Collins and David Cerdeño "Listening to Dark Matter" *Interdisciplinary Science Review.*

9. See https://projects.ift.uam-csic.es/p4uu/exhibition-listen-to-dark-matter/ (Accessed: 29 August 2023).

10. The "Language poets" or "L-A-N-G-U-A-G-E poets" emerged in the 1970s in the USA and were a loosely connected community of writers who engaged critically with each other's work and often cultivated their own means of literary production.

11. Her book *Clairvoyant Journal*, originally published by Angel Hair in 1974, brought these texts together. On the occasion of the exhibition *Breaking News from the Ether* curated by Sebastian Plutot and Frank Bauchard at La Panacée in Montpellier (2014). The text was edited and republished by Bat for the *Go Words!* Residency. See https://www.enrevenantdelexpo.com/2014/06/15/dernieres-nouvelles-ether-art-by-telephone-recalled-la-panacee-montpellier/ and https://vimeo.com/88430301 which give accounts in French of the works at the exhibition that aimed to explore the role of electromagnetic and other invisible energies within artistic practice (Accessed: 08 August 2023).

12. See "Hannah Weiner on Public Access Poetry 12-29-77" https://www.youtube.com/watch?v=DF0IoXUGkKU (Accessed: 29 August 2023).

13. Evidence for this in the archive of the author held at the Harry Ransom Center in Austin Texas, include notes taken during public talks on astrophysics. See https://norman.hrc.utexas.edu/fasearch/findingAid.cfm?eadid=00019 (Accessed: 30 January 2024). See also Adam Guy, (2016), "'that's a scientific fact': Christine Brooke-Rose's Experimental Turn" *The Modern Language review,* 111 (4).

BIBLIOGRAPHY

Bailey, Ain. (2024). 'Tone Poem' London: Café Oto

Bailey, Ain. (2023). 'Adventures in C.A.S' https://on.soundcloud.com/RNmue (Accessed: 30 January 2024)

Bennett, J. (2001). *The Enchantment of Modern Life: Attachments, Crossings, and Ethics,* Princeton: Princeton University Press

Bonet, N. (2016) 'Sonification of Dark Matter: Challenges and Opportunities', *Proceedings of the Sound and Music Computing Conference,* Hamburg: Germany http://hdl.handle.net/10026.1/8035

Brooke-Rose, C. (2007) *The Christine Brooke-Rose Omnibus: Four Novels: Out, Such, Between, Thru.* Manchester: Carcanet Press Ltd.

Brooke-Rose, C. (1965) 'Dynamic Gradients', *London Magazine* 4, pp. 89 – 96.

Collins, R. (2023). *Parameters for Understanding Uncertainty (P4UU).* Available at: https://projects.ift.uam-csic.es (Accessed: 29 January 2024).

Collins, R and Adam Matschulat. (2023). 'Energies not Forms not Figures', *Parameters for Understanding Uncertainty* [vinyl]. London: Flaming Pines (forthcoming)

Collins, R. (2023) *Listening to Dark Matter* [Exhibition]. Exhibition Space, Autonomous University of Madrid, Spain. March 09, 2023 – April, 26, 2023. Available at: https://projects.ift.uam-csic.es/p4uu/exhibition-listen-to-dark-matter/ (Accessed: 30 January 2024)

Combahee River Collective (1983), 'The Combahee River Collective Statement.' *Home Girls: A Black Feminist Anthology,* New Brunswick: Rutgers University Press pp. 264 – 274

Clinton, R. A, (2012) *Spectral Conversions: James Merrill and Hannah Weiner,* New York: Palgrave

Daggett, C. N. (2019). *The Birth of Energy: Fossil fuels, thermodynamics and the politics of work.* Durham: Duke University Press.

Darlington, J. (2017). 'A Non-Euclidean Novel: Christine Brooke-Rose's Such and the Space-Age Sixties', *Journal of Modern Literature,* 40 (2) pp. 147 – 164

Durgin, Patrick (2004) 'Introduction. Avant-Garde Journalism: Hannah Weiner's Early and Clairvoyant Journals' https://library.ucsd.edu/speccoll/m504/index.html (Accessed: 30 January 2024)

Emejulu, A. (2022), *Fugitive Feminism*, London: Silver Press.

Goldman, J. (2001) 'Hannah=hannH: Politics, Ethics and clairvoyance in the Work of Hannah Weiner', *differences a journal of feminist cultural studies*, 12(2), https://doi.org/10.1215/10407391-12-2-121 pp. 121 – 168

Guy, A. (2016). "that's a scientific fact': Christine Brooke-Rose's Experimental Turn' *The Modern Language review*, 111 (4)

Haraway, D. (2016). *Staying with the Trouble: Making Kin in the Cthulucene,* Durham: Duke University Press.

Hejinian, L. (1991). 'The Person' *Poetics Journal* (issue 9).

Hejinian, L. (2000). *The Language of Inquiry,* Berkeley: University of California Press.

Henderson, L. D. (2013). *The fourth dimension and non-euclidean geometry in modern art,* 2nd edition, London: MIT Press.

Hunt, B. (2002) 'Lines of Force, Swirls of Ether' in Bruce Clarke and Lynda Darlrymple Henderson (eds.) *From Energy to Information: Representation in Science, Art, and Literature*, Stanford University Press, pp. 99 – 113.

Jordan, J. (2018). 'Indeterminate Brooke-Rose', *Textual Practice*, 32(2), pp. 265–281.

Kahn, D. (2016). *Earth Sound Earth Signal.* Los Angeles: University of California Press.

LaBelle, B. (2018). *Sonic Agency: Sound and Emergent Forms of Resistance.* London: University of Goldsmiths Press.

McKittrick, Katherine. (2015). *Sylvia Wynter: On Being Human as Praxis.* Durham: Duke University Press.

Mody, C. C. M. (2005) 'The Sounds of Science: Listening to Laboratory Practice', *Science, Technology and Human Values* 30 (2) https://doi.org/10.1177/0162243903261951

Mould, O. (2023). 'From globalisation to the planetary: Towards a critical framework of planetary thinking in geography', *Geography Compass,* 17 (9) https://doi.org/10.1111/gec3.12720

Moten, F. and Wu Tsang. (2016). *Who Touched Me?, London: If I Can't Dance, I Don't Want to Be Part of your Revolution.*

Plutot, S. and Frank Bauchard. (2014) *Breaking News from the Ether* [Exhibition] La Panacée: Montpellier.

Randall, L. (2015) *Dark Matter and the Dinosaurs.* London: Harper Collins.

Rosa, Sophia, K. (2023) *Radical Intimacy.* London: Pluto Press.

Spivak, Gayatri Chakravorty. (2003) *Death of a Discipline.* New York: Columbia University Press.

Weiner, H. (1990), *Weeks,* West Lima: Xexoxial Editions.

Weiner, H., Rae Armantrout et al. (1991) 'Symposium on the Person', *Poetics Journal* (9) ed. Barrett Watten and Lyn Hejinian.

Weiner, H. (1992) Fast, USA: United Artists Books.

Weiner, H. (2014) *Clairvoyant Journal*, 2nd edition, Dijon: Les presses du réel

Woolf, V. (1978) Moments of Being: Unpublished autobiographical writings of Virginia Woolf St Albans: Triad/Panther Books.

NANNA HAUGE KRISTENSEN

My Mother's Voice

"... and I was lifted, wet and bloody, out of my mother, into the world,
screaming

and enough."
Ocean Vuong, *Time is a Mother* (2022, p. 51)

The living room windows turn toward the forest. Outside the birch trees are naked. It is winter, the gloaming hour. My mother has poured herself a glass of red wine. She always does that at five o'clock. We sit on the couch and watch the darkness grow outside. I ask her:

Mum, how do you remember the sound of your mother's voice?
She thinks for a moment.
Mother's voice was calm. A pleasant voice. But I find it hard to describe.

Yes. How to describe a voice? The materiality of the sound. Its hidden sensibilities. When we listen to a voice, we listen to "... the somatic and the semantic qualities in parallel: to the corporeal texture, to the movements in melody and rhythm, but also to meanings and relations, all at the same time. It is a daring methodological endeavor to explore the voice in all its physical, corporeal, mental, emotional, and sensible realities," writes the German voice anthropologist Ulrike Sowodniok (2020, p. 126). And maybe the endeavor of exploring the voice of a mother is particularly daring.

It is among the first sounds we hear – the sound of our mother's voice. Yet unborn, we are already listeners of the surrounding world. The French audio-psycho phonologist Alfred A. Tomatis describes how the mother's voice is transmitted by bone oscillation of the spine directly to the ear of the foetus. According to him the most modifying quality within the symbiosis of the mother and the unborn baby is the sound of the maternal voice. It becomes the leading quality for the sensory development of the child (Tomatis cited in Sowodniok 2016, p. 53). And so, our mother's voice resonates within even before we are lifted out into the world. It continues to do so as we grow into life. We attune to it. We listen to it. We react to it. We embody it. We carry it as an echo deep inside – even when we are separated from her. Even when we do not wish to hear it.

"Whose voice am I not listening to?" asks the sound artist Cathy Lane in her audio paper *Listening and not listening to voices* (2017). Here she reflects upon what listening and hearing means – and how the Sound Art Canon can become more pluralistic, more inclusive.

With an undertone of irony in her own voice, Lane narrates how there is a voice she tends to ignore: the voice of her mother – ageing and gradually sliding into dementia. It is difficult for her to listen to that voice. It is, as she states, "emotionally difficult." She "does not need those unresolved emotions." She needs time to be able to devote her attention to her sound art. The work that her mother has never understood, nor heard – although she features in a lot of it.

Maybe the changes in her mother's voice, the vulnerability, the undertone of decay, makes it particularly difficult for Lane to listen. However, it inspires her to raise the question: "How can we listen to the voices of those who are in the periphery? The largely unheard. Or heard but ignored or misunderstood."

Back in the living room my mother asks me:

> *Do you think voices are passed down from one generation to the next?*
> Me: *I don't know. Does your voice remind you of your mother's?*
> Mum: *Does yours remind you of mine?*
> Me: *I wouldn't mind if it did. I like your voice. I liked it when I was a child, too.*

THE TOUCH OF VOICE

To contextualize what you are about to read I will share a personal experience.

My mother and I are in another living room. This one is in the apartment where I live with my partner and our child. Outside there is not a forest, but a giant maple tree covered with leaves. I am in deep despair. I still love my partner, but I have grown so small in the life that we share. I try to push it away, but a feeling keeps surfacing: An urge to leave our relationship. I share my thoughts with my mother. She replies: *But without him you have nothing.*

The words come quickly, with no breath in between. I recognize my mother's voice, but it is as if my maternal ancestors are speaking through her. Maybe this is one of the ways voices are passed down from one generation to the next. As transgenerational convictions: *Without him you have nothing.*

The experience ignites a curiosity within me about female voices, maternal voices. The voices we spring from. Therefore, years later, I ask different people, mainly women, to record their mother, asking her the same question as I asked my own mother in the beginning:

Mum, how do you remember the sound of your mother's voice?

My intention is to capture three generations of female voices in one recording although only two of them will be physically present. However, not everyone is able to record their mother and the project transforms. Instead, I receive recordings and texts where the contributors themselves recall their mother's voice. Memories, associations, analogies, sensory impressions, sonic qualities, textures. The ways to perceive a voice are various.

To the voice anthropologist Ulrike Sowodniok the quality of sound is like that of touch: reciprocal and passing: "It wraps itself around us and embraces us with a nearness that gives us no choice but to study the entanglement rather than the object. And from this reciprocal embrace it asks: *What is … – there?*" (Sowodniok cited in Voegelin 2020, p. 109).

Yes, what is … – there? Remembering our mother's voice – what kind of touch do we sense? A caress? An embrace? An itch? A stroke?

As I mentioned earlier, we are profoundly touched by that voice. Its audible and inaudible aspects wrap themselves around us and move deep beneath our skin. Therefore, recalling our mother's voice can be an intimate – and perhaps provocative – act that stirs unresolved emotions.

A CARRIER BAG OF MATERNAL VOICES

To gather citations about maternal voices carries an emotional dimension. But there is another dimension tied to it. This has to do with the freedom to express oneself as a woman – and to be heard. To be included.

My grandmother's voice was calm. Pleasant, my mother tells me. I never met my grandmother. What I know about her is that her favorite flowers were dahlias, she had a strained relationship with her mother, and she wanted an education, but she never got one. She left no traces of her inner life. And when I sense or imagine her, there is a silence emanating from her. *She was a good listener*, my mother adds.

Cathy Lane shares how her mother, like so many carers, has spent her life subserving others, sacrificing her own desires, comfort, time and energy. Like Lane, I wonder how overheard voices can become audible. Incidents in my own biography have given me an awareness about the women who lived before me and their restricted expressions; their positions of being muted. Sometimes

I even feel what could be a reverberance of their quietness in my own voice. It sneaks in as a hesitation.

In her essay "The Carrier Bag Theory of Fiction" (1989) the American writer Ursula K. Le Guin replaces the idea of the spear as the earliest human tool with that of the carrier bag. By doing so, she shifts the way we look at humanity's foundations from a narrative of domination to one of gathering, holding, and sharing. To Le Guin, the carrier bag becomes a method for storytelling itself. Unlike the shape of the spear, the carrier bag allows for messy, entangled, collective and nonlinear stories.

I like to think of the following pages as a carrier bag. A kind of vessel that provides space for female voices – the voices of mothers and of daughters. Maybe they speak together on the page? Singing, a safe harbor, bedtime stories, a dry cloth, the sun. This carrier bag talks of ambiguity and love, about connection and longing.

Although the voices remain silent on the page, recalling them is a way of giving attention to them: a way of listening. Listening reminds us how recognition is affected by the sense of being heard, as Brandon LaBelle writes. He continues by stating, "Listening addresses the unsaid, attending to that which is withdrawn or repressed. In doing so, it further opens an extremely important sense for the not-yet, for what remains to be said" (2021, p. 7).

The maternal voices contained here do not speak with their own words. Instead, they are represented through the subjective sensations of their daughters. However, to remember them allows them to become present – to be heard for a moment – both the voices of the mothers who are still alive and the ones who are no longer with us, but still resonating.

How do you remember the sound of your mother's voice?

— The sound of my mother's voice is beige in color. Her name was brown.

— In the afternoons, while she sewed
and mended clothes, and I did my homework,
we talked. Her voice was calm and soft.
She was a good listener.

— When I hear my mother's voice on the phone,
I turn the volume down. It's like a dry cloth.
The words are wrung out, with no moisture.

— I often miss my mother. Sometimes, if my mother is very calm
or maybe tired, when she isn't busy with things, she can speak
in a voice that is deeper and slower than normal. And this voice
gives me … it nourishes me. When she talks like that, it's not
about something that's going to happen.

— Sometimes my mother's voice has suppressed laughter.
Listening to her makes me feel like she's the one who knows
me best in all the world. She speaks not just to my ears,
but also to my inner core.
Her voice is the sun. And now, after fleeing the war, I can say
"the Danish sun" because I don't hear it so often. But when
it comes, it brings great warmth.

— My mother's voice is deeper when she
speaks her mother tongue, which is French.
When she speaks Danish, her voice
sounds more tense, shriller and harder.
She has almost always spoken Danish
with me. When I was very little, I think she
spoke French. But then at some point,
she switched. It's a bit hard for me to understand why she chose to do so – to speak
a language with me that wasn't her own, a
language she had only just learned.

— My mother's voice was restrained
and full of longing. I didn't know what
she was longing for.

— I describe my mother's voice, and while I do that, I listen to
my own voice. Our voices are similar in a way I hadn't
realized. When I think of my mother's voice, I can sense her
whole person. Her skin when I was young was warm and
softly damp, freckly and salty. Her skin reminds me of matzo
ball soup, the kitchen growing humid from the soup on
the stove, the air salty. My mother was not really someone
who made soup ... but she emanated salty, warm humidity.
Broth-like. But most of all, it's the taste I feel close to.

— Sometimes, when I can't remember my mother's voice,
I try listening deep inside.

— It's the first time I've called my mother in the three months
I've been here. I'm standing in the hallway, by the door
to the bedroom of my dad and his new wife. The black Bakelite
telephone can't be moved. "Have you seen the moon?"
she asks. I lean towards the warmth that radiates toward my chest.
There are seven thousand kilometers between us.
The phone hisses and crackles in my ear.

— I've called my mother on the phone when I've been happy,
excited, sad, or frustrated. Maybe I also needed her help.
Her voice is warm and deep, unchanging. A safe harbor. Calm.
Always as expected.

— My mother's voice sounded one way when she had been drinking,
and another when she had not.

— The voice of my mother was deep and dark like velvet.
It could be loud and shrill when she was angry.
When she sang, her voice sounded round and jazzy.
After she got cancer of the oesophagus ... she kind
of lost that voice. She can still sing, but not with the same
soft fullness I remember from my childhood.

— My mother's voice. Hard, grey and a bit tired. But ...

— When we were in the summer house and my mother looked down at
the sea, her voice turned soft and warm.

— I remember my mother's voice from the TV set in our living room.
She is an actress and gave voice to a cartoon. Not only to one
character, but to all of them. It was a five-minute cartoon which was
on the program every evening at quarter past seven. She was
playing two rabbits — Ushko and Zupko and a villain — Jarac the Goat.
I listened to the cartoon like I was bewitched. It was my personal
little horror movie. I hated the transformation of her voice, especially
to the evil goat Jarac. At the end of the cartoon there was a song —
and my mother, famous for being tone-deaf, was then singing in those
voices, which was the peak of terror.

The other memory of her voice from my childhood is a dear one.
I remember her voice singing to me when I was sick, with a temperature.
She would always sing two partisan war songs.
One was called *In the middle of the rifles and bayonets*, and the
other one was *On the Konjuh mountain* about burying a dead comrade.
Those songs were so tragic and gloomy, but strangely soothing.

    — She could certainly be mild. My mother was good at making
gloves. She was a glovemaker and received special orders
from people with hand deformities. When she came home, she
told us how she had invented a clever kind of button system
for people who had unusual hands. She described the gloves in
detail and passionately. She took great pride in making them
so that they were the "crème de la crème." When she felt proud
of herself, her voice had a very distinctive sound.

— My mother's voice is questioning.
So eager to ask that she asks again, before
she hears the answer.

— Her voice, the tone she uses, the words she speaks, their
volume, their rhythm ...

— I'm trying to remember. They all talked, all those sisters together ...
She spoke half-Polish, half-German. My mother was very musical.
She played the piano; her father played the violin.
Her voice was probably melodious. I've never thought about it like that.
We talked at dinner, but I didn't talk one-to-one with my mother.
Not like I talk with you. It was different back then.

— My mother always laughed a lot.
At school performances she laughed easily and very loudly,
with tears, and she would throw herself back. She tried to stop
herself. She thought it was too much, but she couldn't help it.

— When it was time for my nap, and the shutters were closed to keep
out the sun, I would lie down on my bed and my mother would sit next
to me and tell me stories. When she ran out of the stories she knew,
I insisted that she made up new ones. That's one of the first memories
I have of my mother. Her soft, slow voice.

83

— My mother's voice is like pine needles.
Soft, but it can become pointy and prickly.

— I remember my mother as gentle. Sometimes she could raise her voice,
but I hardly ever remember her angry. She must have been, though, before she
and my dad got divorced. Back then her voice had a different tone.

— I find it hard to remember my mother's voice
when she was happy. I can't really remember her laughing,
either, although I wish I could. I remember her sigh.

— My mother's voice has become more frail, more nervous.
It's become more and more like my grandmother's voice. Also,
when she sings to my child, it's not quite her voice anymore.
Sometimes I think it's a role she takes on: "Now that I'm older,
I must talk and sing like this."

— My mother's voice is only inside me now. It's there as
laughter, sparkling inside mine.
When I laugh it comes out unexpectedly because our
voices are so different.
She carried a lot of pain in her life, and I've been mad
at her, because it kept spilling over into mine.

But, this laughter, like thousands of tiny bells: a ribbon
of kindness that binds us together.
And maybe it is Death itself that makes it so.

— My mother's voice creaks a bit with age.

— I remember my mother's voice on the phone
when I was little, and she called home to say goodnight.
It spoke to a soft longing within me.

— In the end she hardly spoke. I read the paper to her. She slept a lot.
We talked about practical things. How she had to lift her legs
when I helped her to the toilet, and when she needed to be washed.
Our conversations weren't about the past or the future. We all
did the same. We didn't talk about what would happen after she was
gone, or about what we were about to lose.

— But ... my most vivid memories of her voice are of her
laughing. I can hear how her eyes fill with tears.

Thank you to all the contributors for sharing their mother's voice: Lisbet Bangsbo Andersen, Line Bangsbo, Marie Suul Brobakke, Synnøve Brøgger, Astrid Hald, Lotte Forchhammer, Alaa Kassab. Stine Korsgaard, Stine Louring Nielsen, Alejandra Basualto Pearcy, Sandra Lori Petersen, Maria Rakel, Hanne Refslund, Charlotte Bastholm Skjold, Kirstine Lindemann Sørensen, Gunni Torp, Michael Ulfstjerne, Hana Vecek, Karen Werner, Marion Werner, and to those who wish to remain anonymous.

A special thanks to my own mother Inge Hauge Kristensen.
Translation: Stine Korsgaard and Billy O'Shea

BIBLIOGRAPHY:

LaBelle, B. (2021) *Acoustic Justice: Listening, Performativity, and the Work of Reorientation.* London: Bloomsbury Academic.

Lane, C. (2017) "Listening and not listening to voices." *Seismograf.* Available at: https://doi.org/10.48233/seismograf1901

Leddy, S. (2019) "We should all be reading more Ursula Le Guin." https://theoutline.com/post/7886/ursula-le-guin-carrier-bag-theory

Le Guin, U. K. (1989) *The Carrier Bag Theory of Fiction. Dancing at the Edge of the World: Thoughts on Words, Women, Places.* New York: Grove Press.

Sowodniok, U. (2016) "Voce en Libertá – Freed Voice: An Applied Anthropology of the Voice." *The Senses & Society.* Vol 11, Issue 1, pp 50 – 59.

Sowodniok, U. (2020) "The Voice" in H. Schulze (ed) *The Bloomsbury Handbook of the Anthropology of Sound.* London: Bloomsbury Academic. pp 111 – 128.

Voegelin, S. (2020) "Pulse" in H. Schulze (ed) *The Bloomsbury Handbook of the Anthropology of Sound.* London: Bloomsbury Academic. pp 107 – 110.

Vuong, O. (2022) *Time is a Mother.* New York: Penguin Press

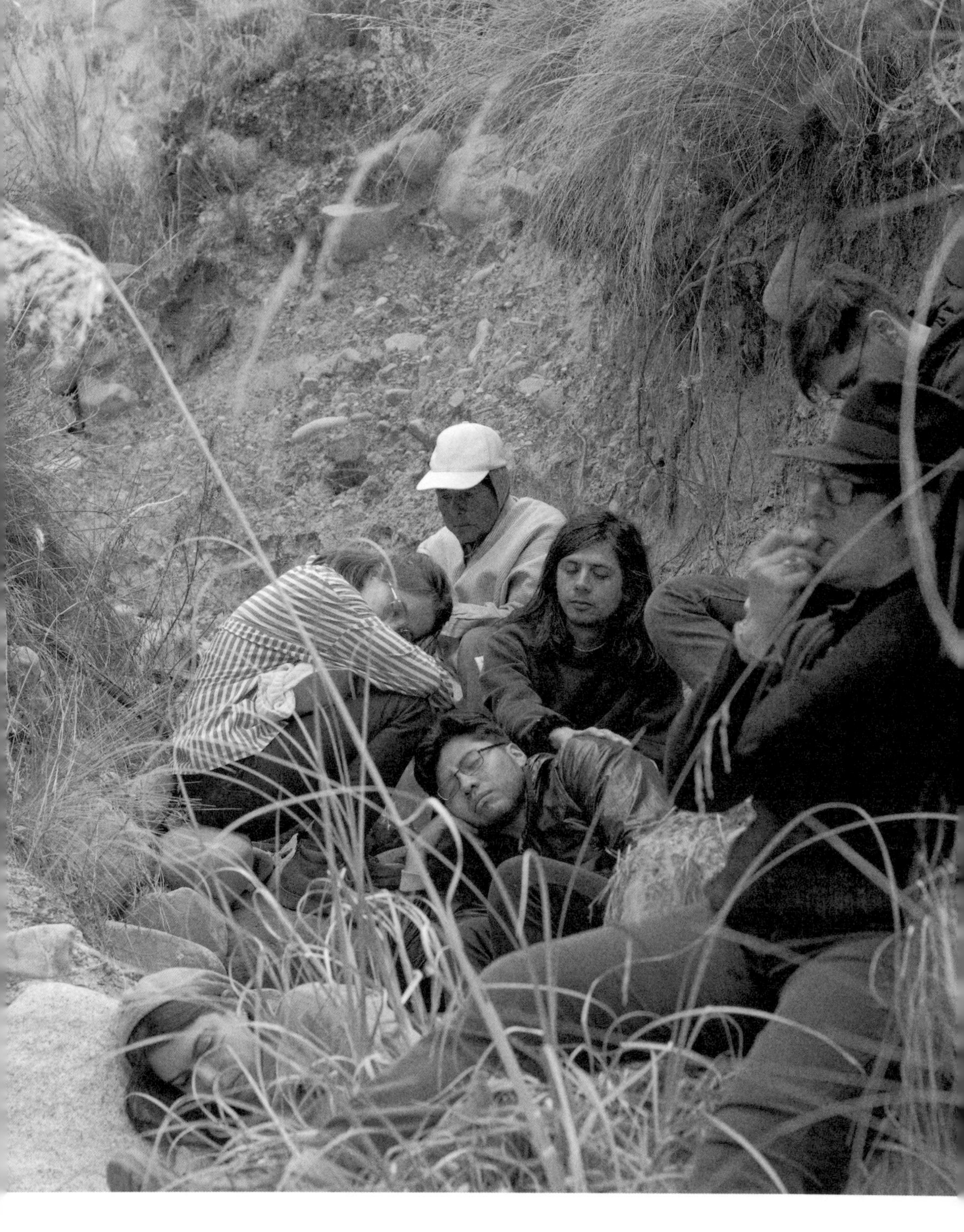

The Listening Biennial brought together 35 participating artists and 30 partner institutions presenting exhibitons, listening situations, talks, workshops and related events. Curated by Rayya Badran, Guely Morato, Luísa Santos and Dayang Yraola, the Biennial sought to create *attentional ecologies* in support of poetic sensing and worlding.

SANTA ANA DE CHIPAYA, BOLIVIA / Ariel Bustamante and German Lazaro, collective listening encounter, following the winds (p. 88).

EDIFICIO ARRONIZ BIBLIOTECA, GUADALAJARA / listening session, Israel Martínez and Ana Lidia M. Domínguez Ruizof in conversation (p. 90).

BAKERIYA SPACE, COLOMBO / creating an intimate listening experience, sharng and reflecting together (p. 90).

SUPERMARGINÁL CAFÉ, BELGRADE / listening sessions over coffee (p. 91).

BALLHAUS OST, BERLIN / The Listening Academy, bringing together participating artists and researchers through somatic listening (p. 92 – 93).

ANIMA PROJECT SPACE, MANILA / collective jam with local artists (p. 94).

CINE TEATRO 6 DE AGOSTO, LA PAZ / live radio session with Yolanda Mamani (p. 95).

REBONKERS, VARNA / live performance and audio mix with experimental musicians Angel Simitchiev and Lucia Udvardyová (p. 96 – 97).

SILPAKORN UNIVERSITY, BANGKOK / curator Dayang Yraola presenting (p. 98).

LYDGALLERIET, BERGEN / listening lounge, exhibition presentation (p. 98).

CZKD CENTER FOR CULTURAL DECONTAMINATION, BELGRADE / presentation with Viktor Vejvoda "Supermarginál café" (p. 99).

LISTEN GALLERY, GLASGOW / soundwalk, listening workshop with Clara Hancock (p. 100 – 101).

BEIRUT ART CENTER / collective listening session followed by open discussion, sharing and reflecting together on sonic experiences (p. 102, 104).

EL CENTRO DE ARTE SONORO (CASO), BUENOS AIRES / exhibition presentation and explorative listening activity (p. 103).

ERRANT SOUND, BERLIN / live performance with Lisa Stewart and Florence Freitag (p. 104).

INSTITUTO CAMÕES, TOKYO / live performance by the artists djsniff and Makoto Nomura, opening the exhibition (p. 105).

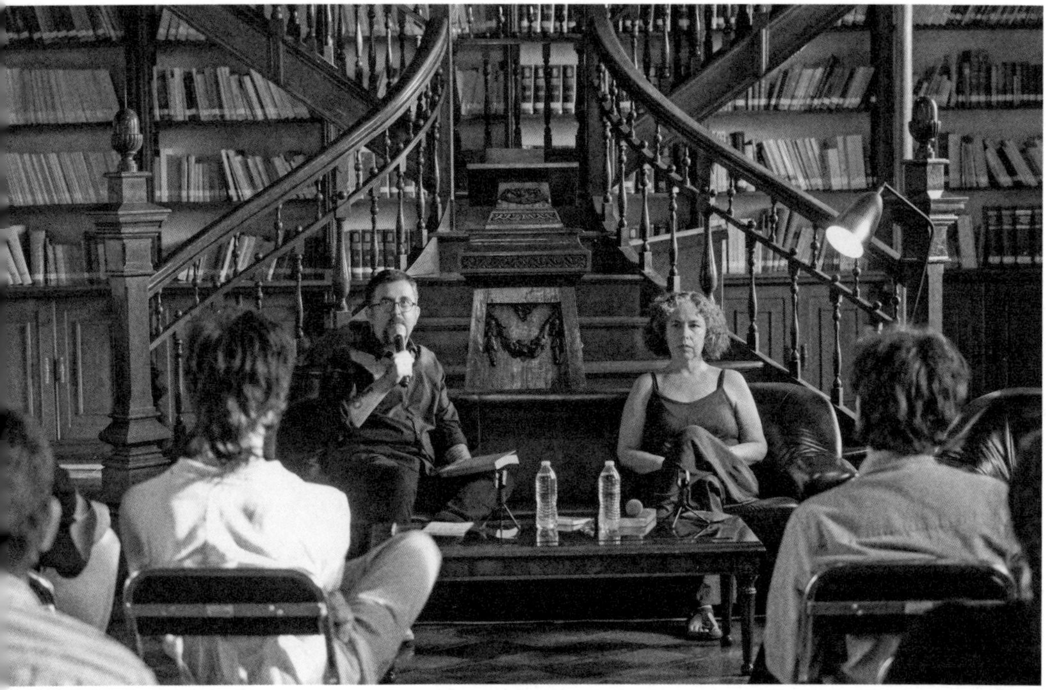

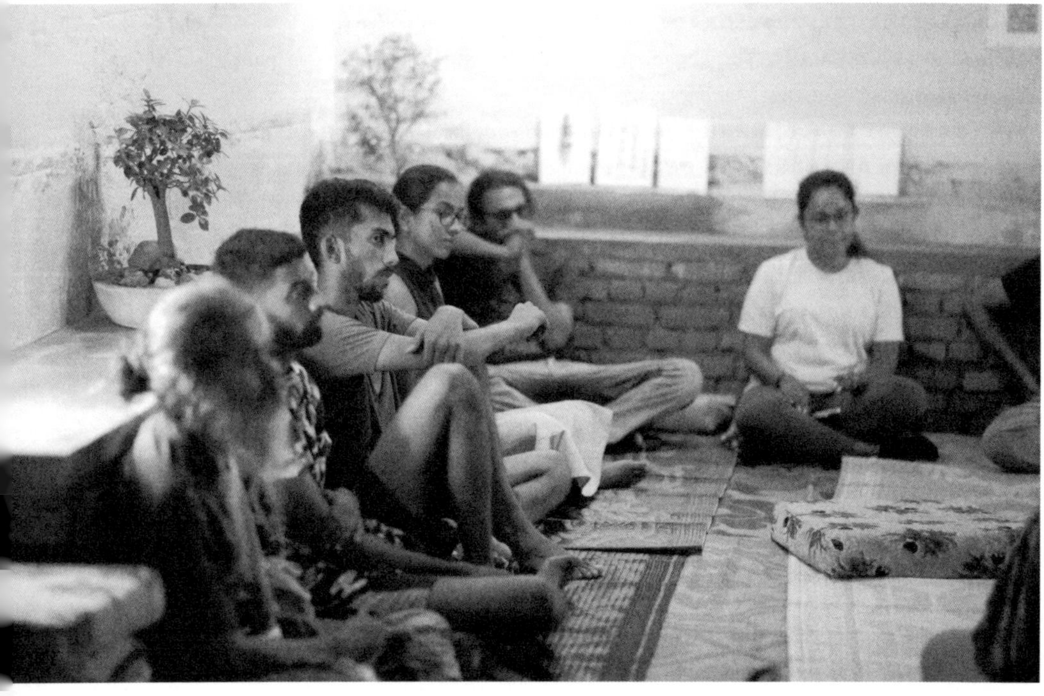

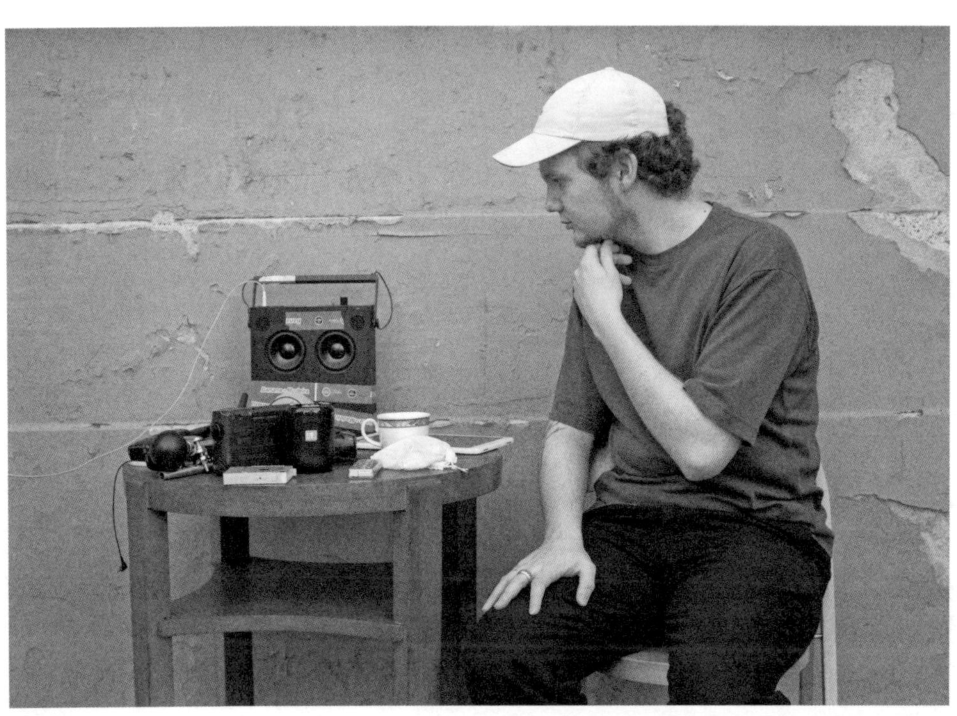

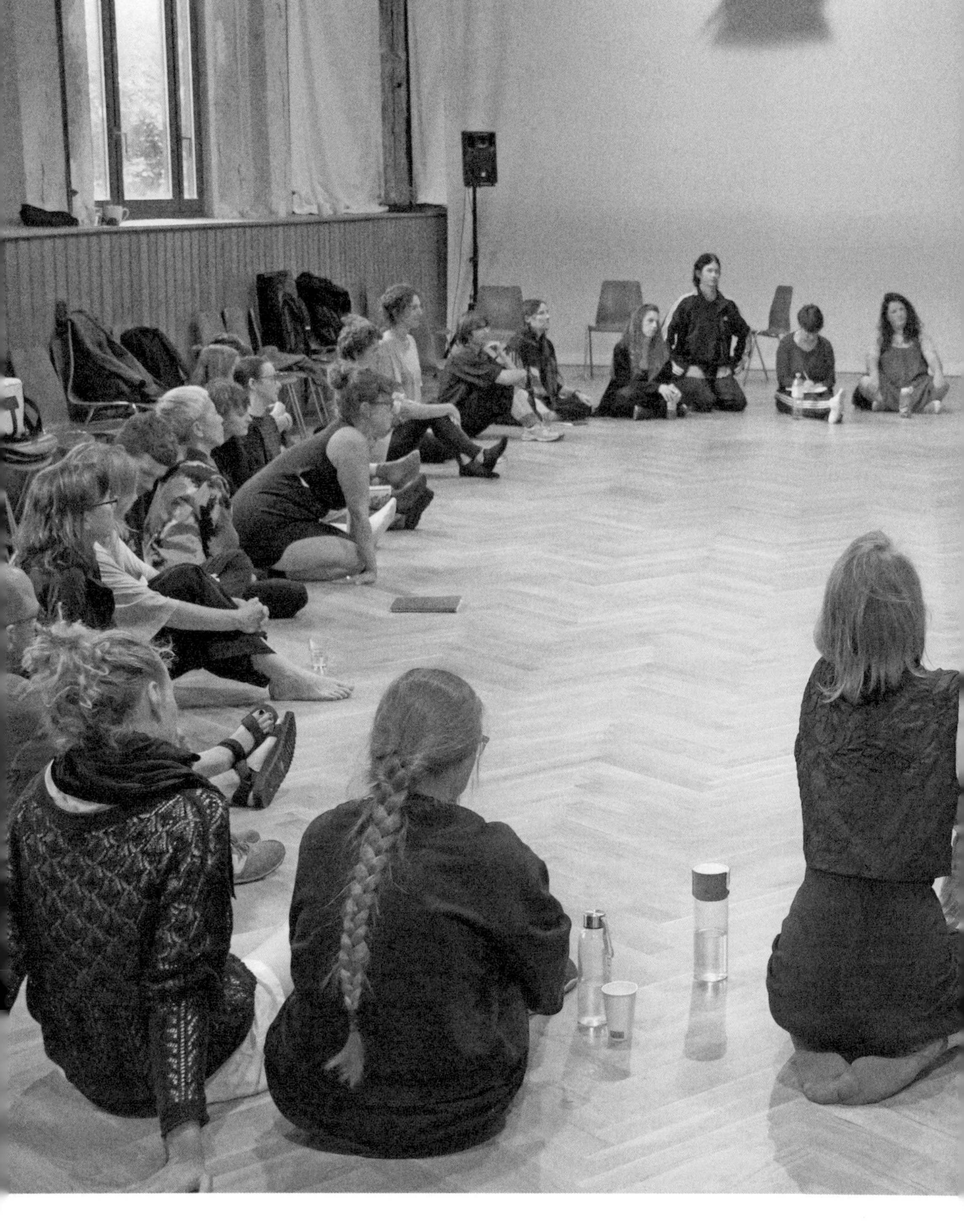

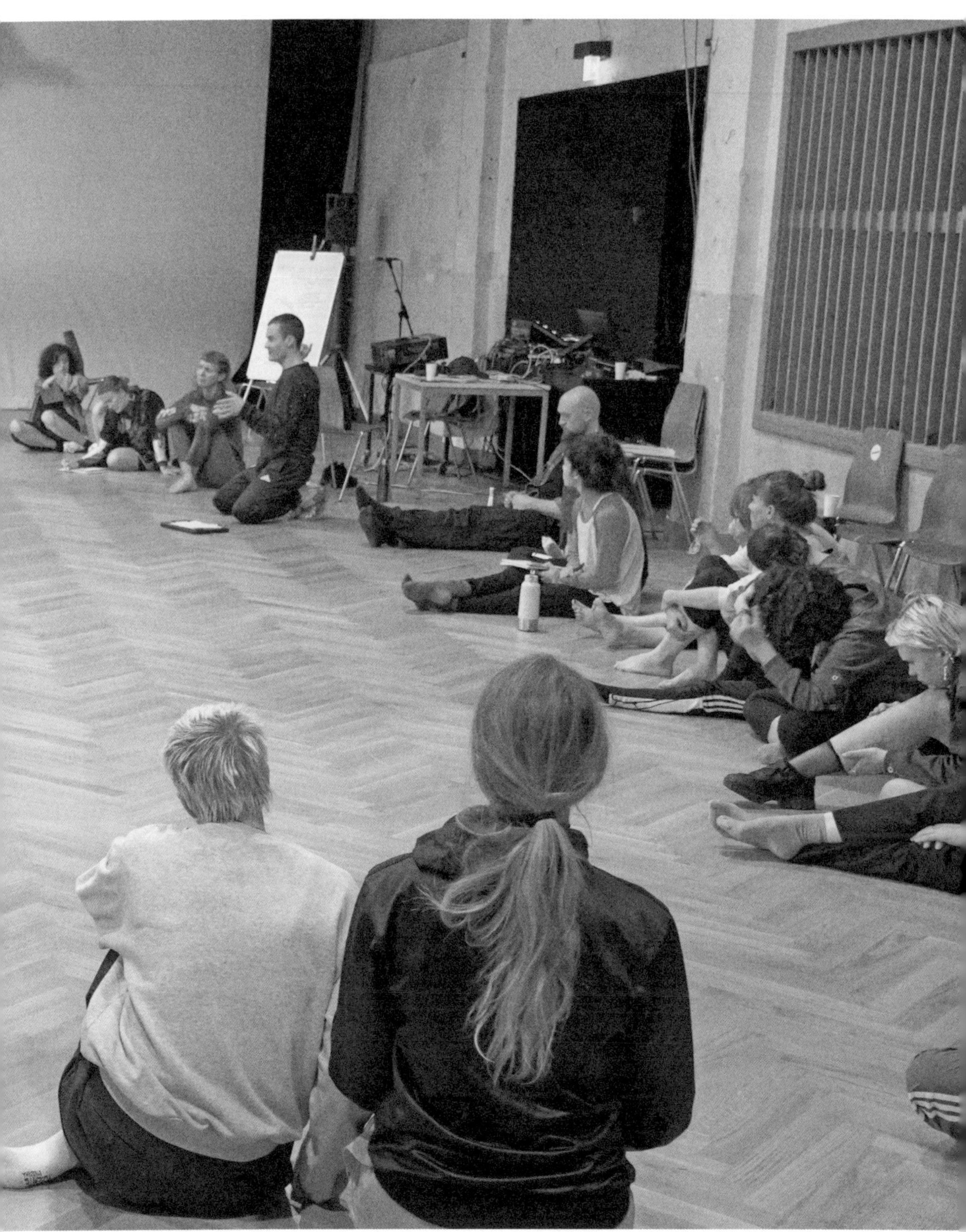

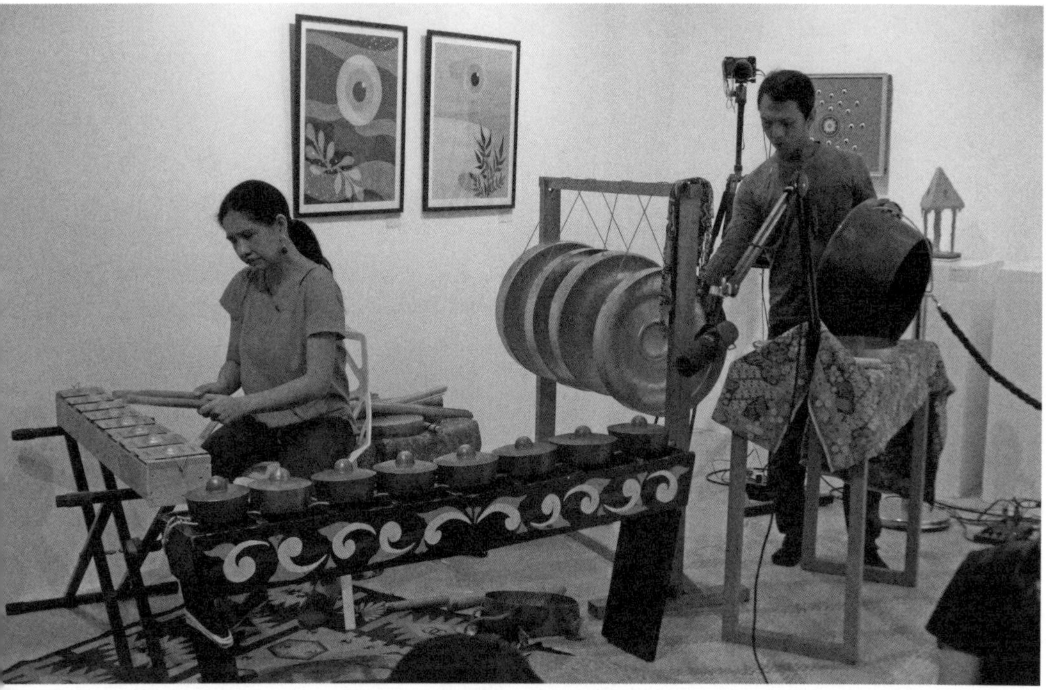

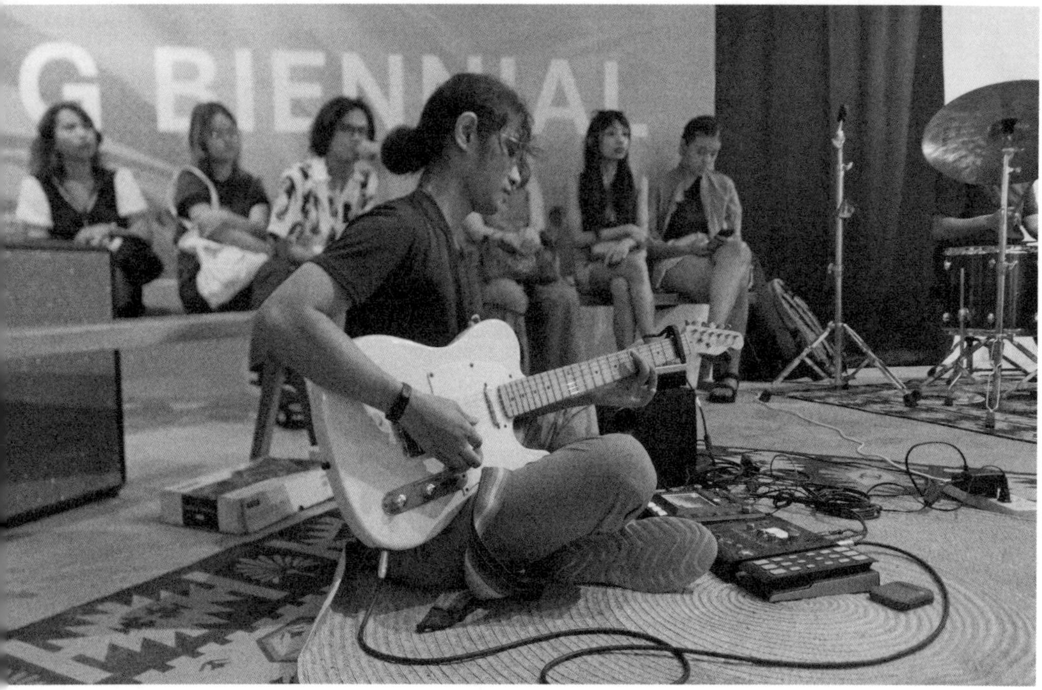

G BIENNIAL

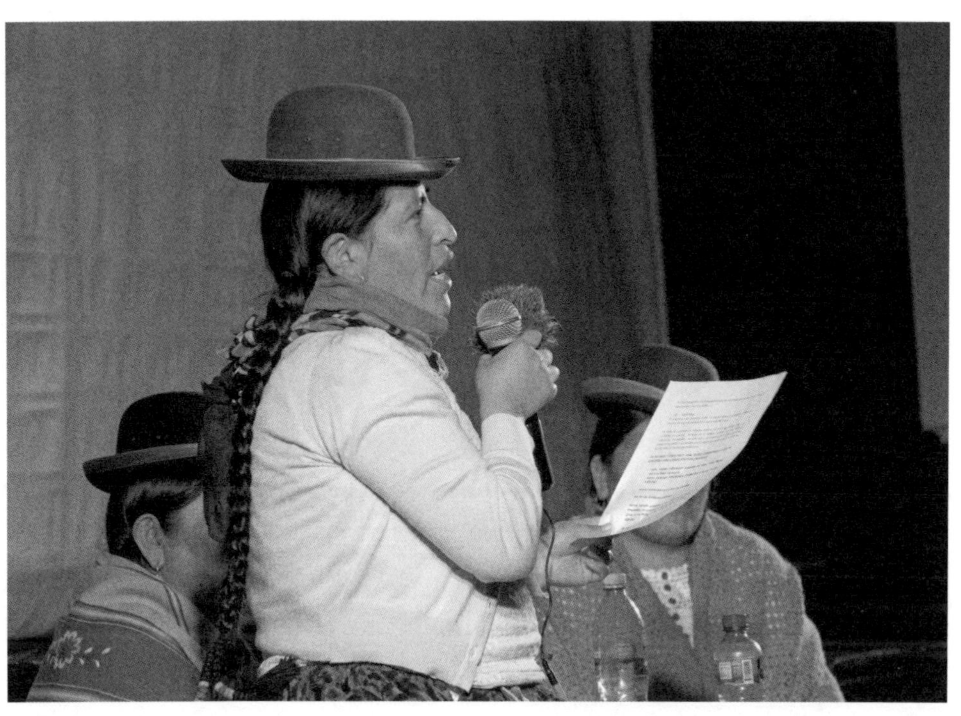

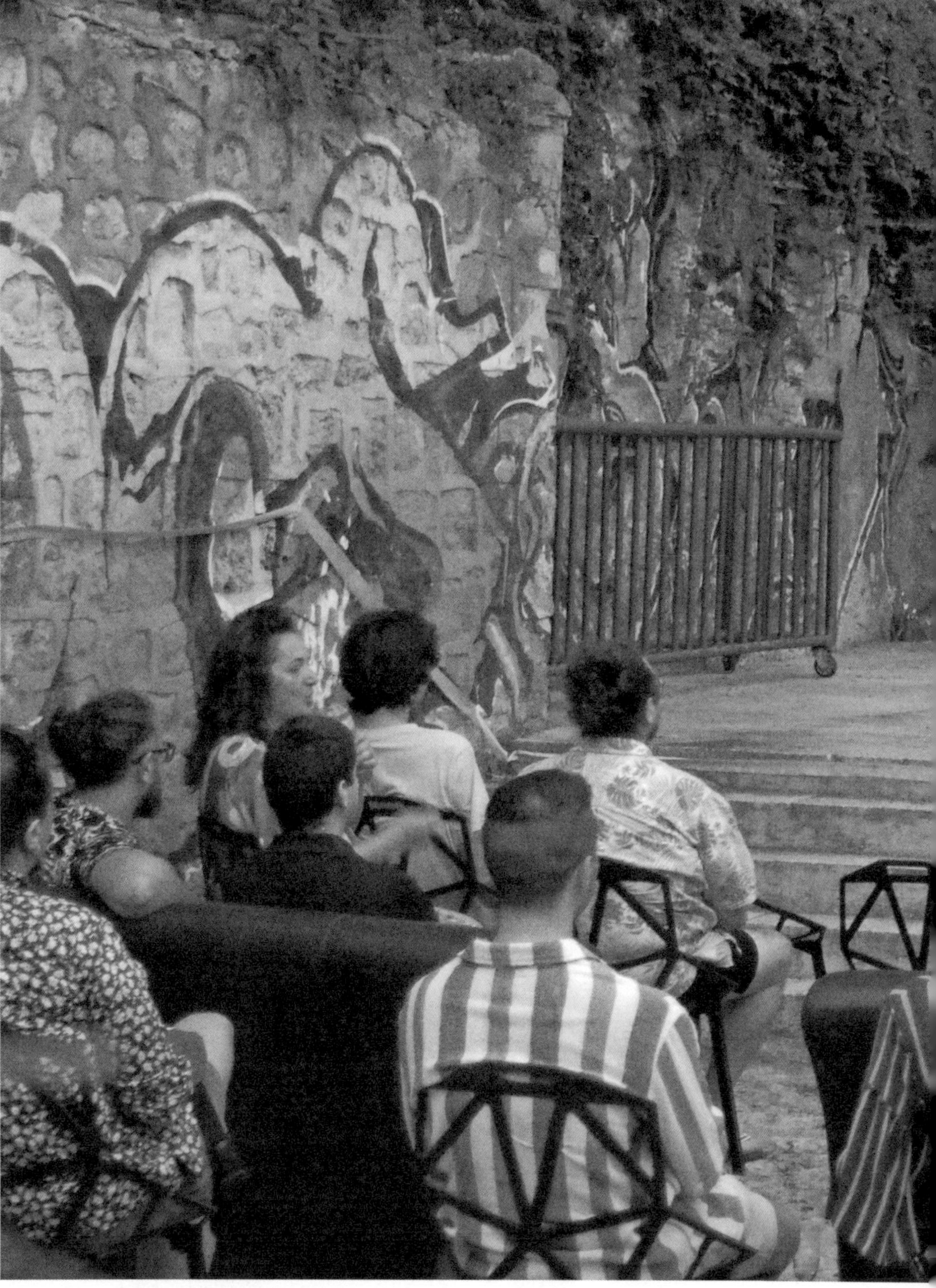

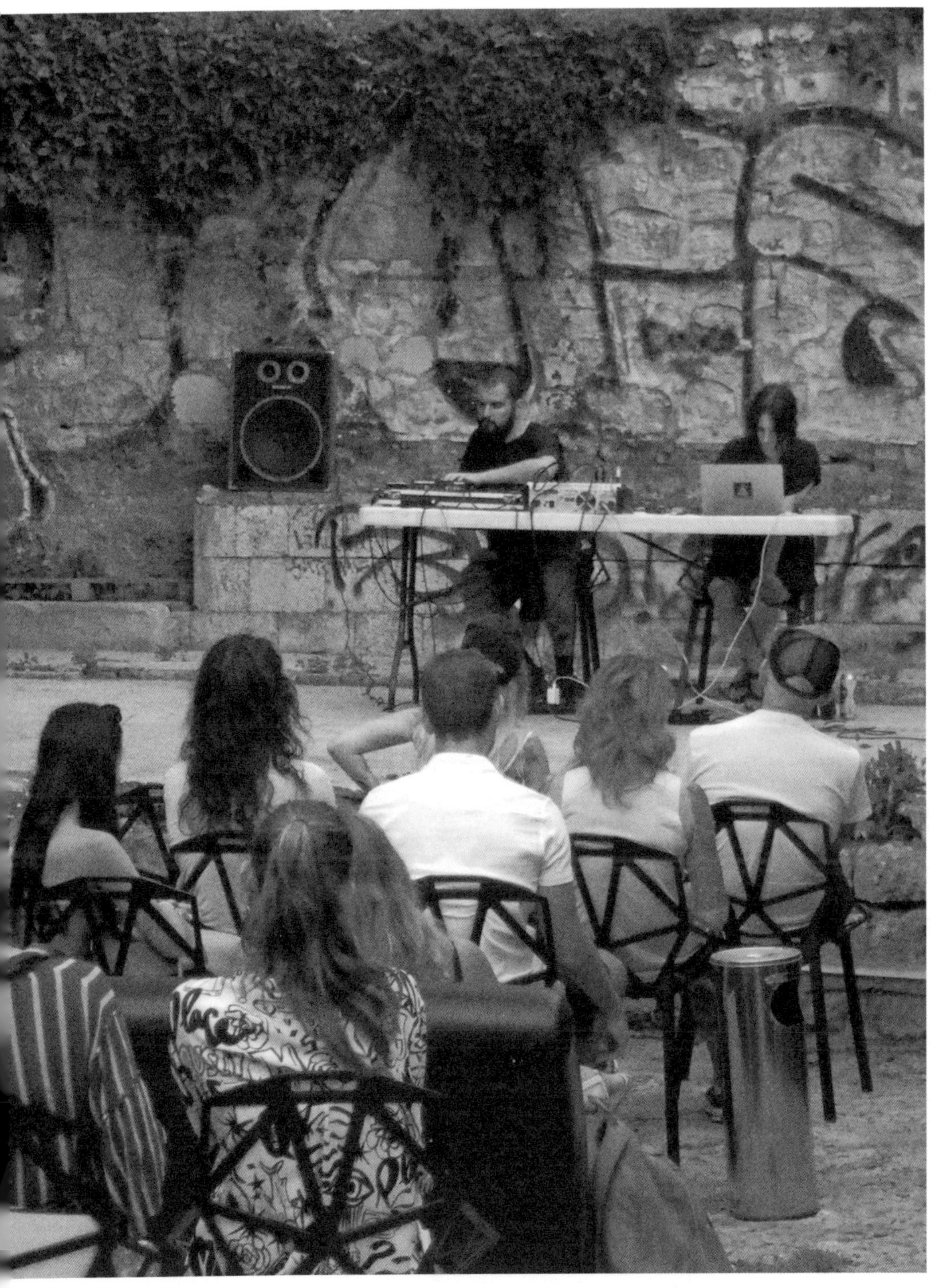

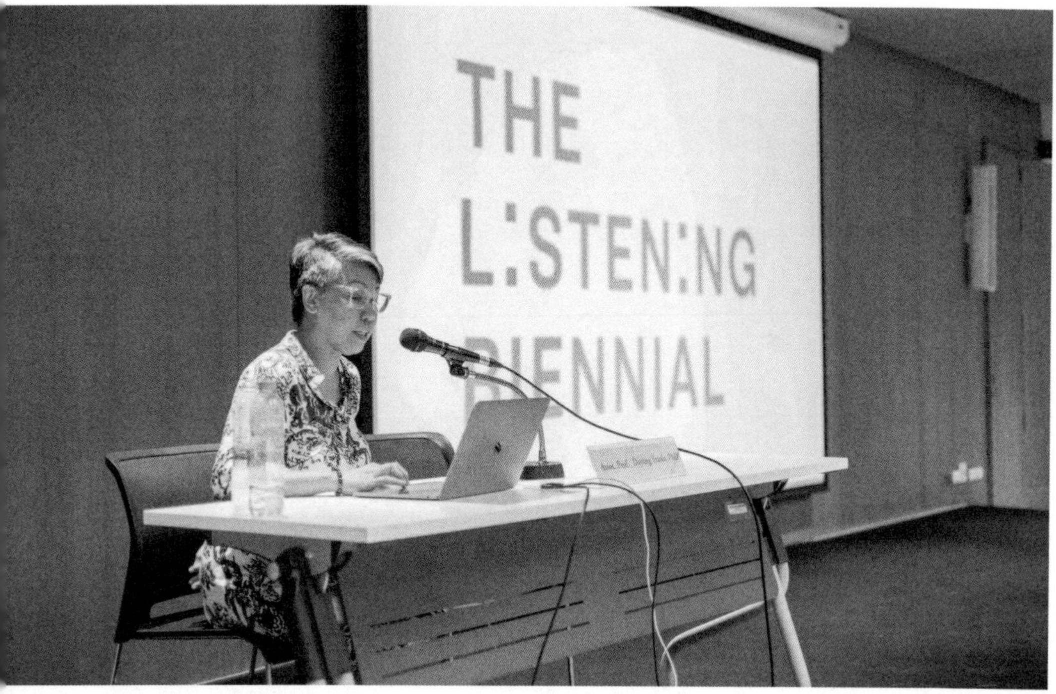

THE
L:STEN:NG
BIENNIAL

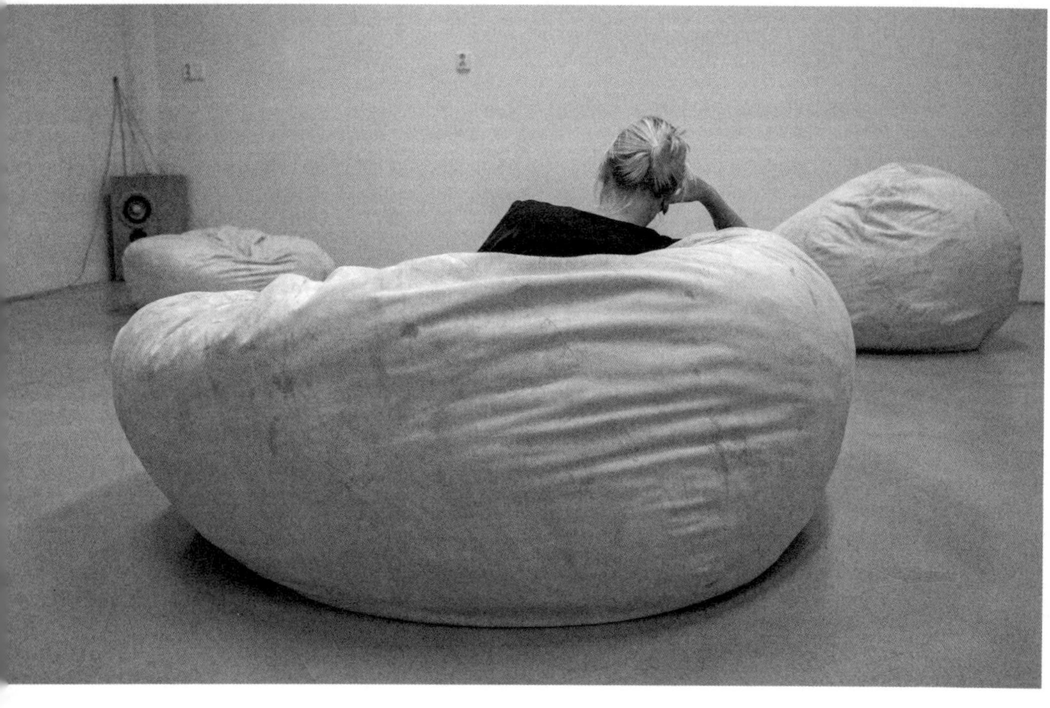

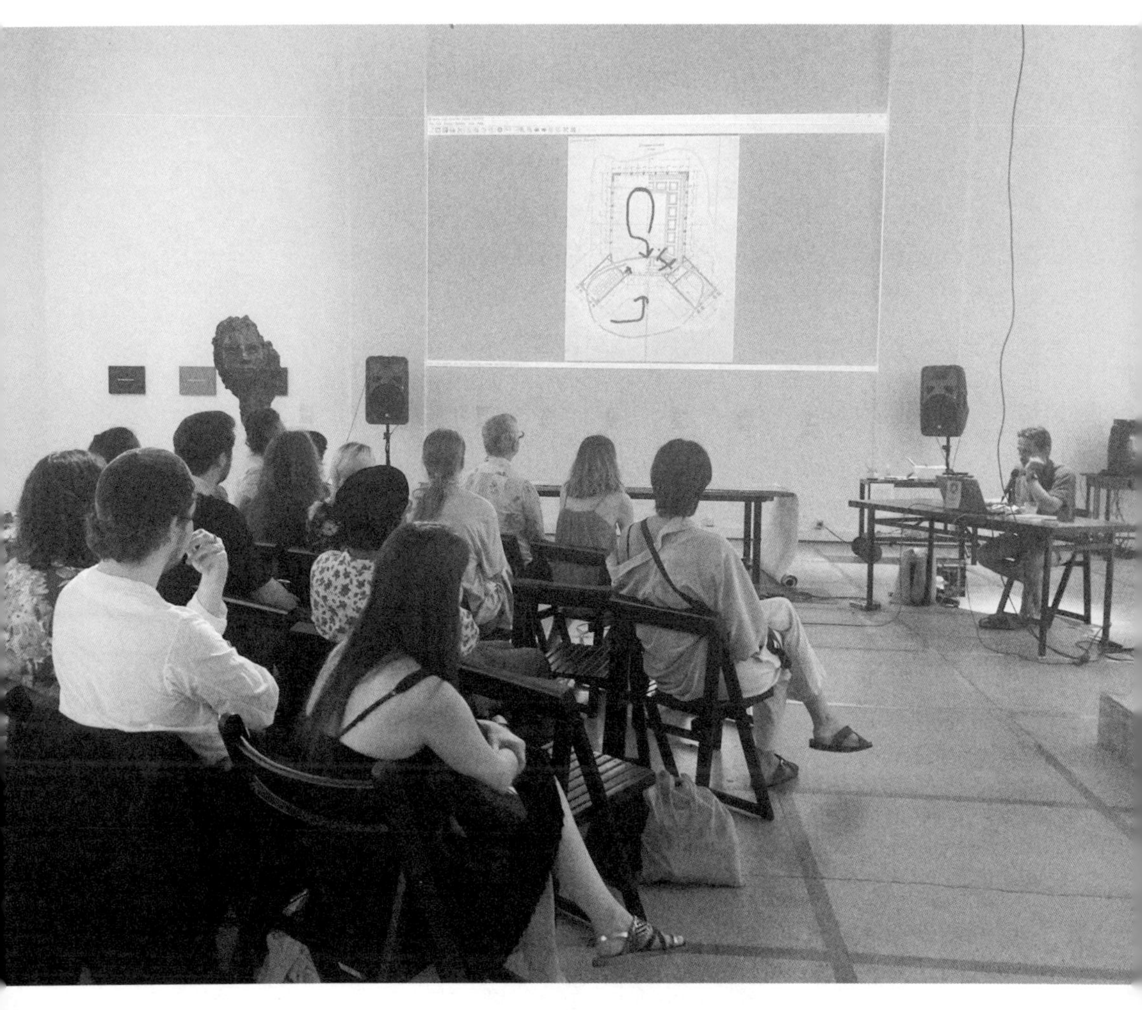

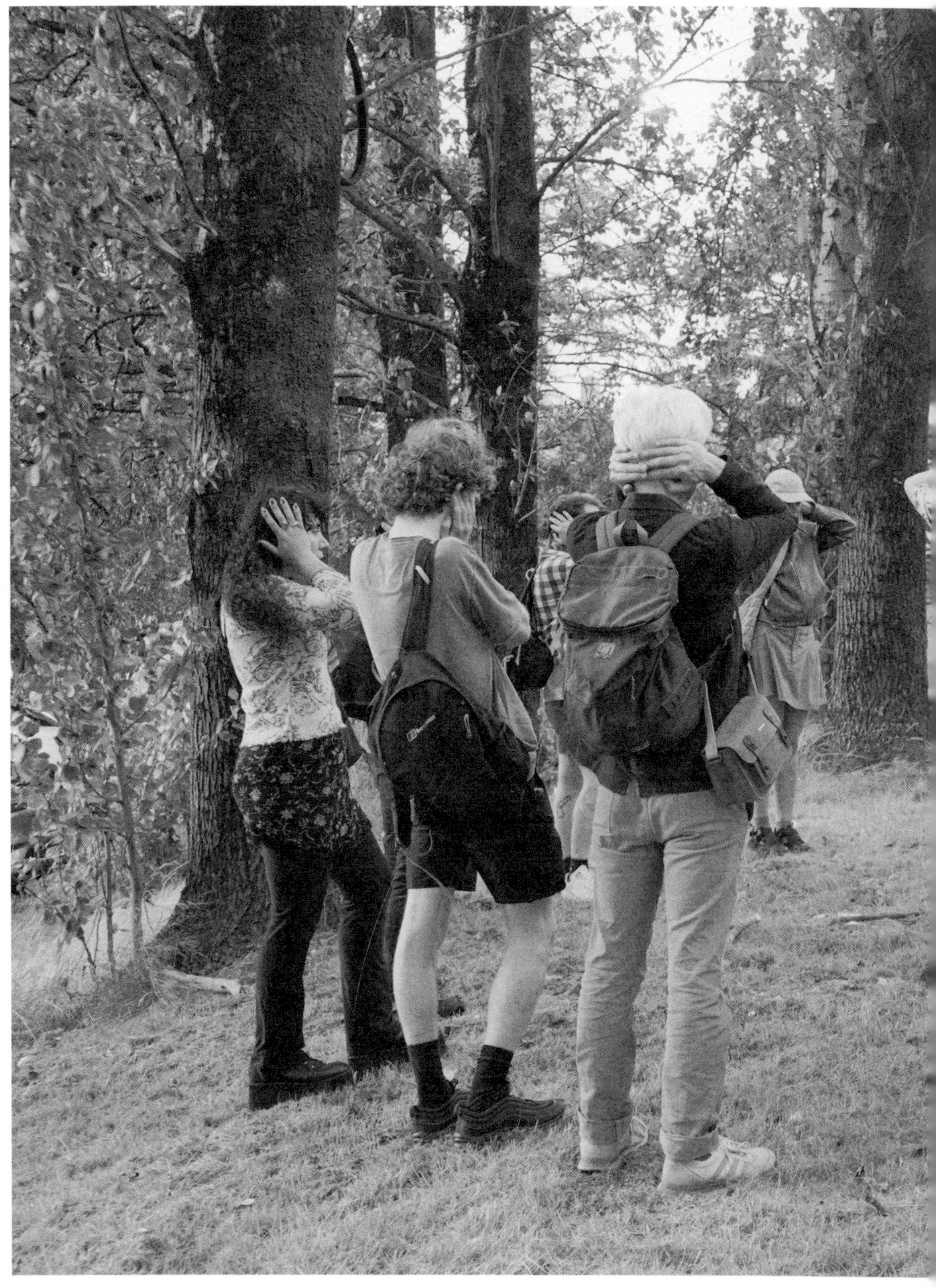

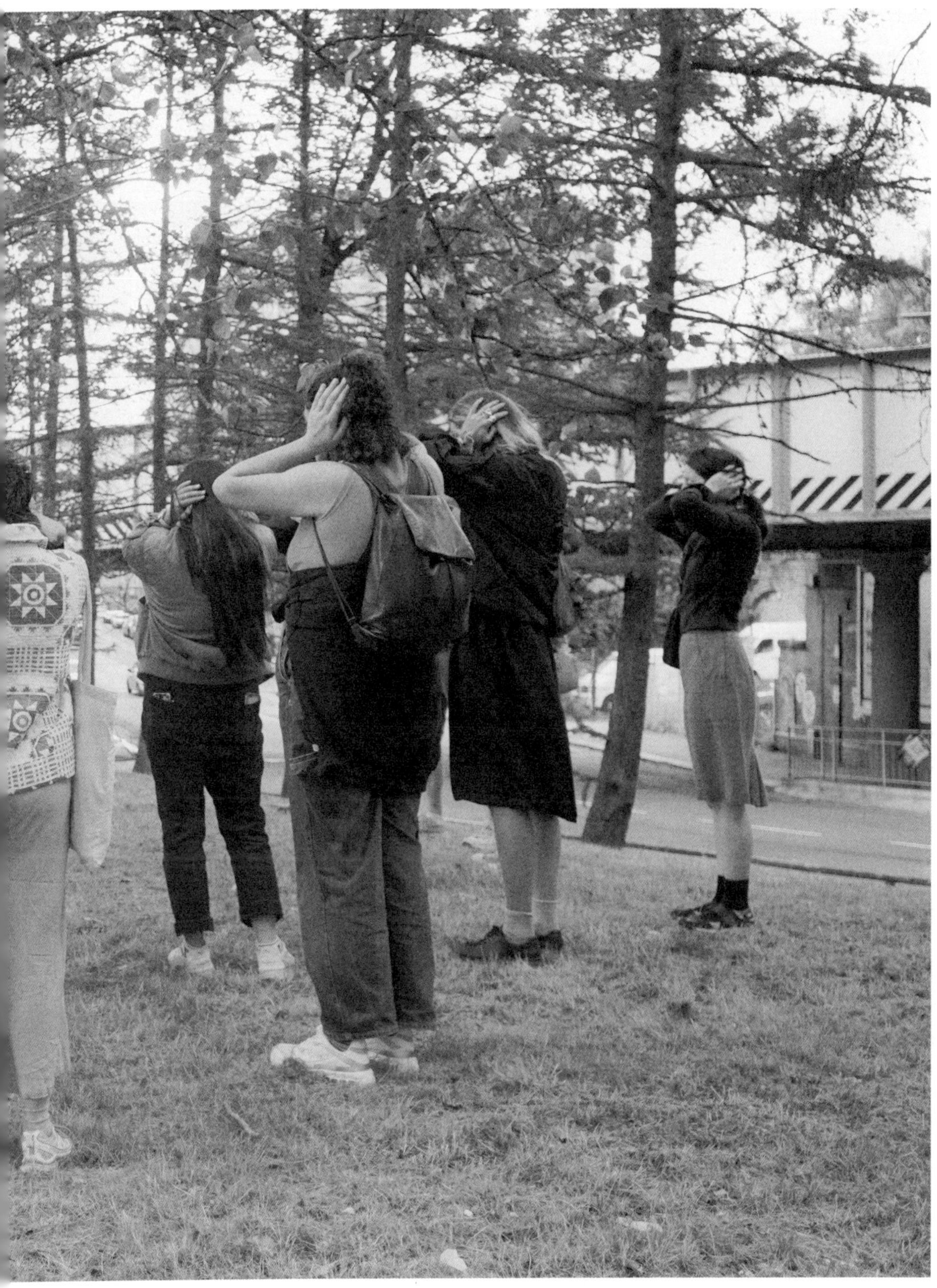

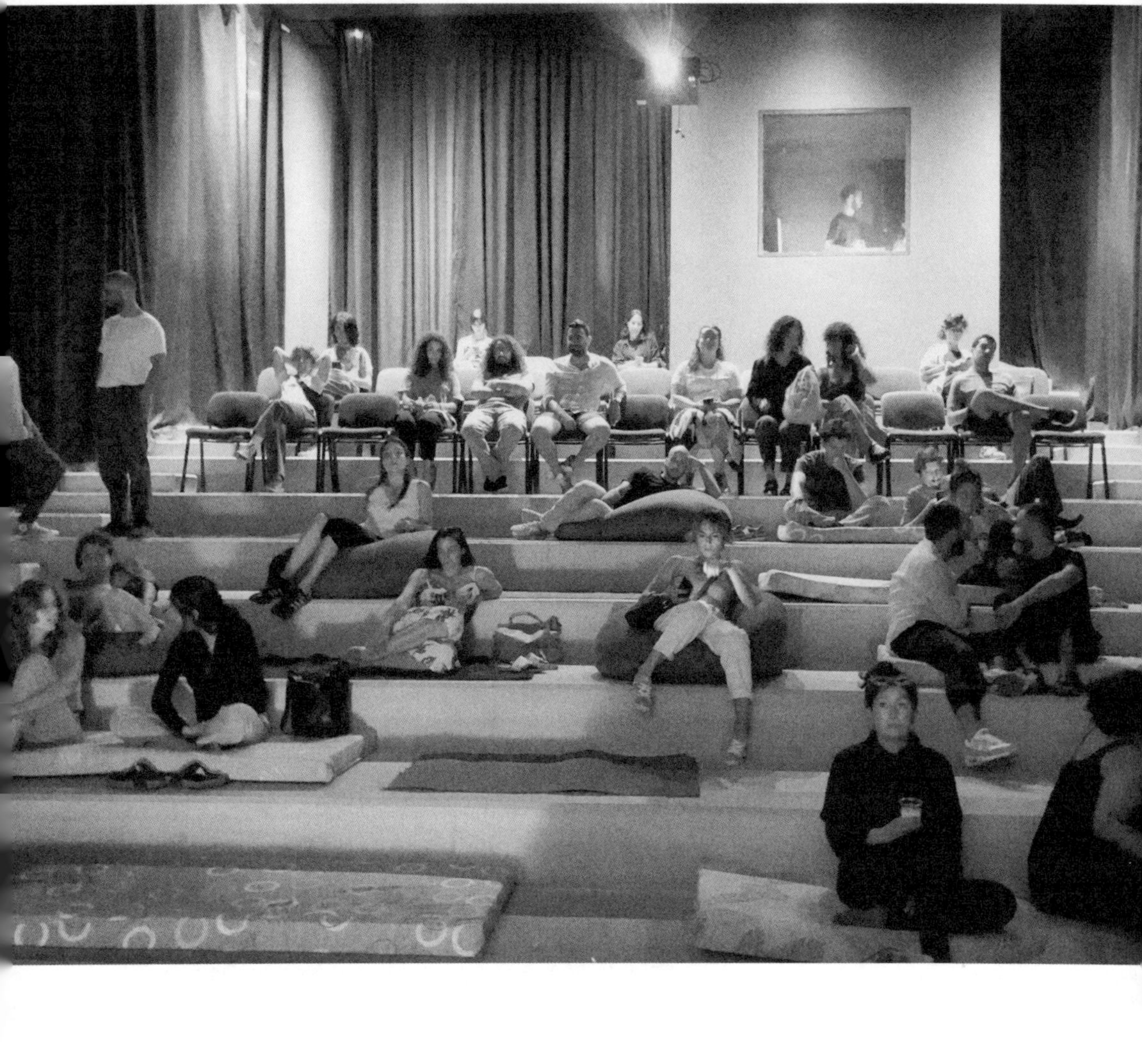

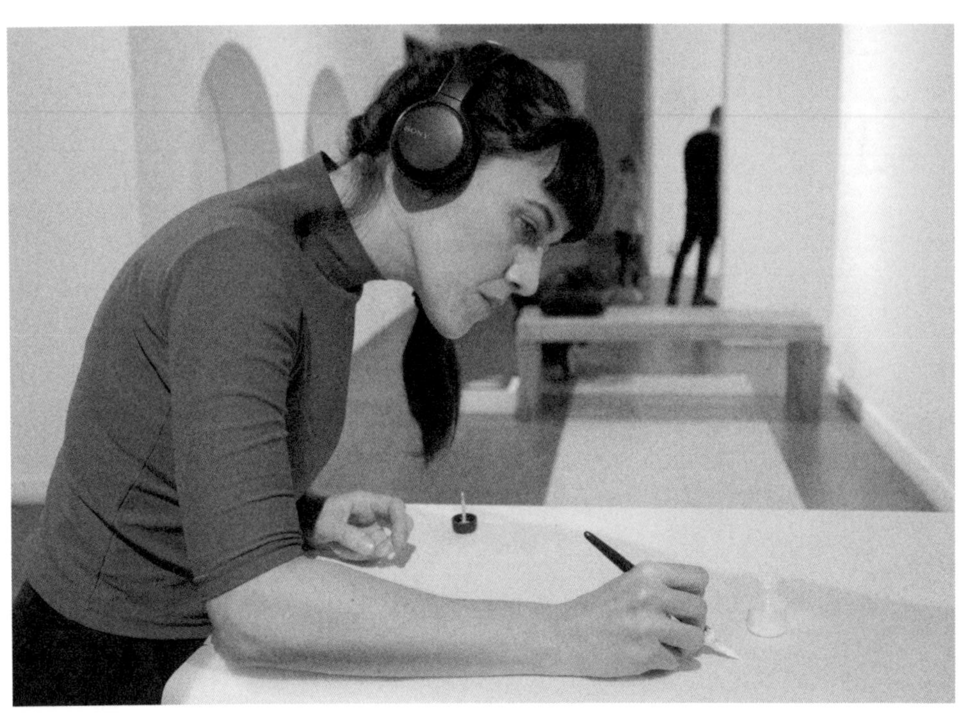

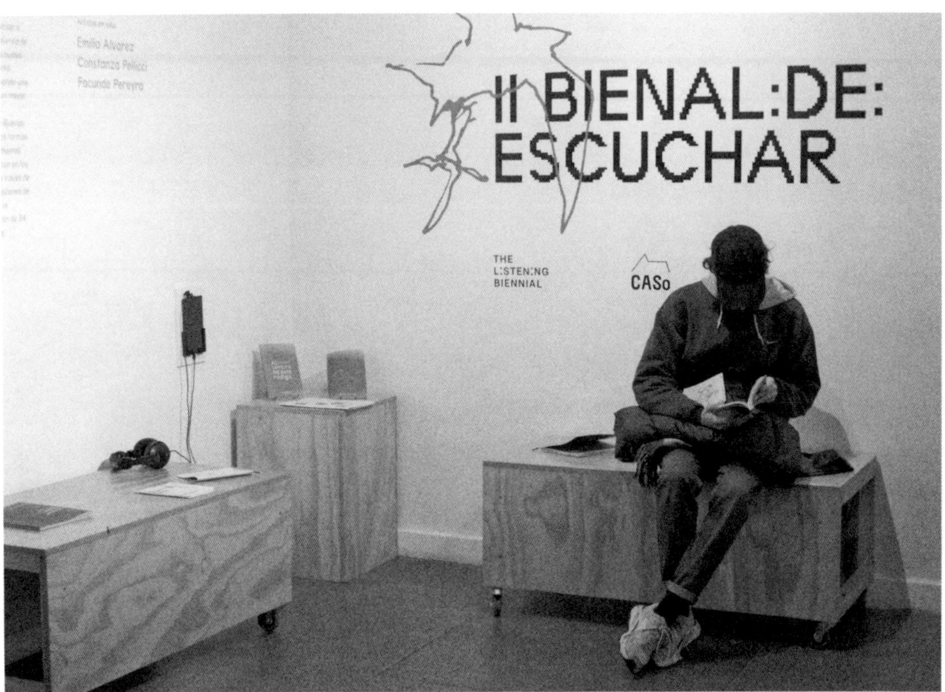
Emilio Alvarez
Constanza Pellicci
Facundo Pereyra
II BIENAL:DE:
ESCUCHAR
THE
LISTENING
BIENNIAL
CASo

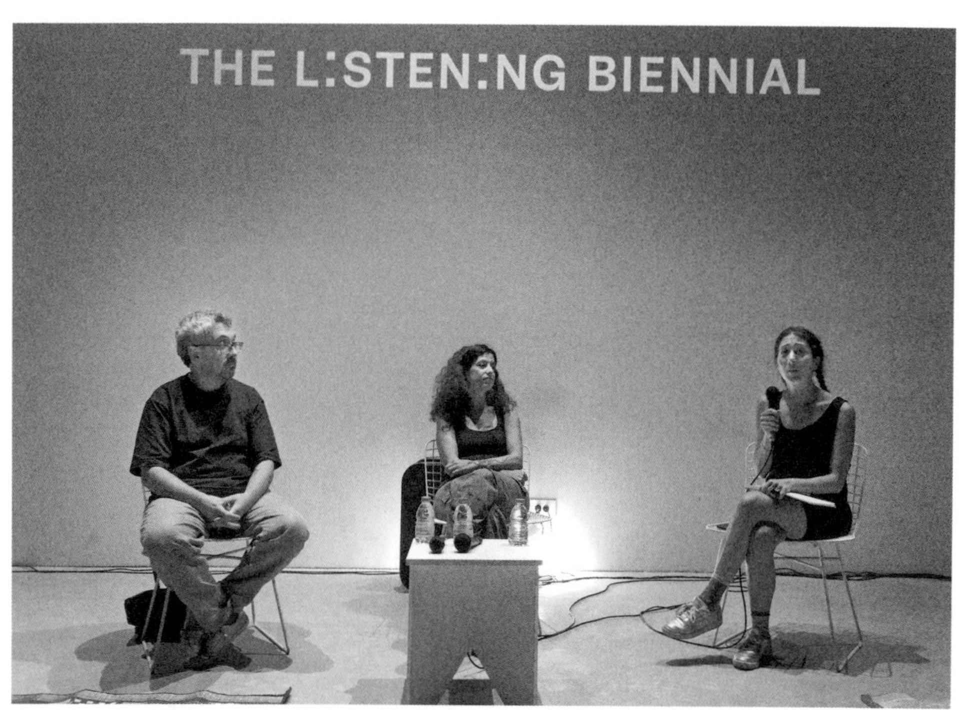
THE L:STEN:NG BIENNIAL

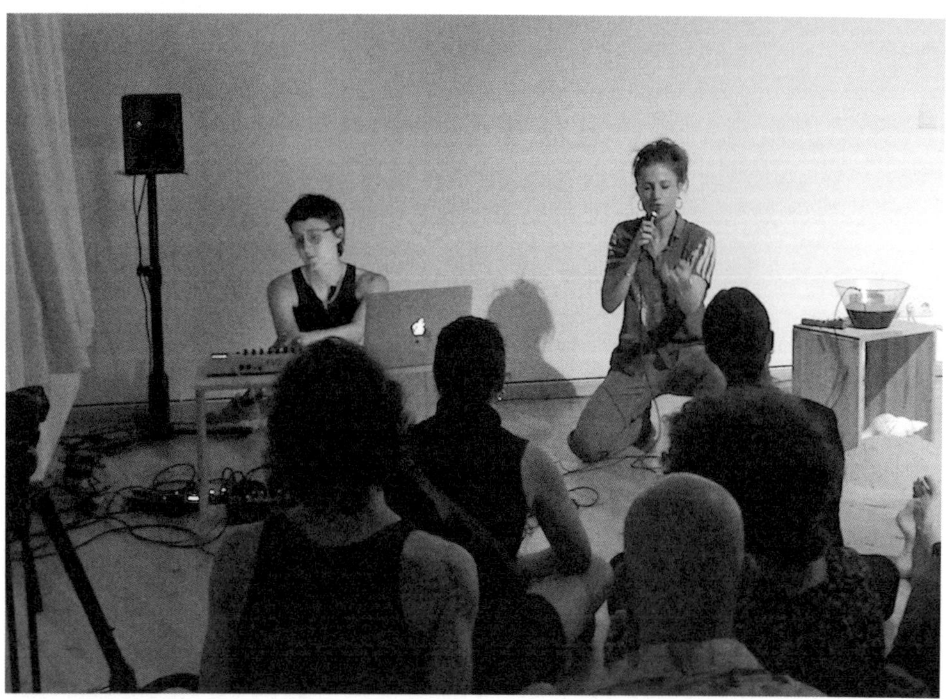

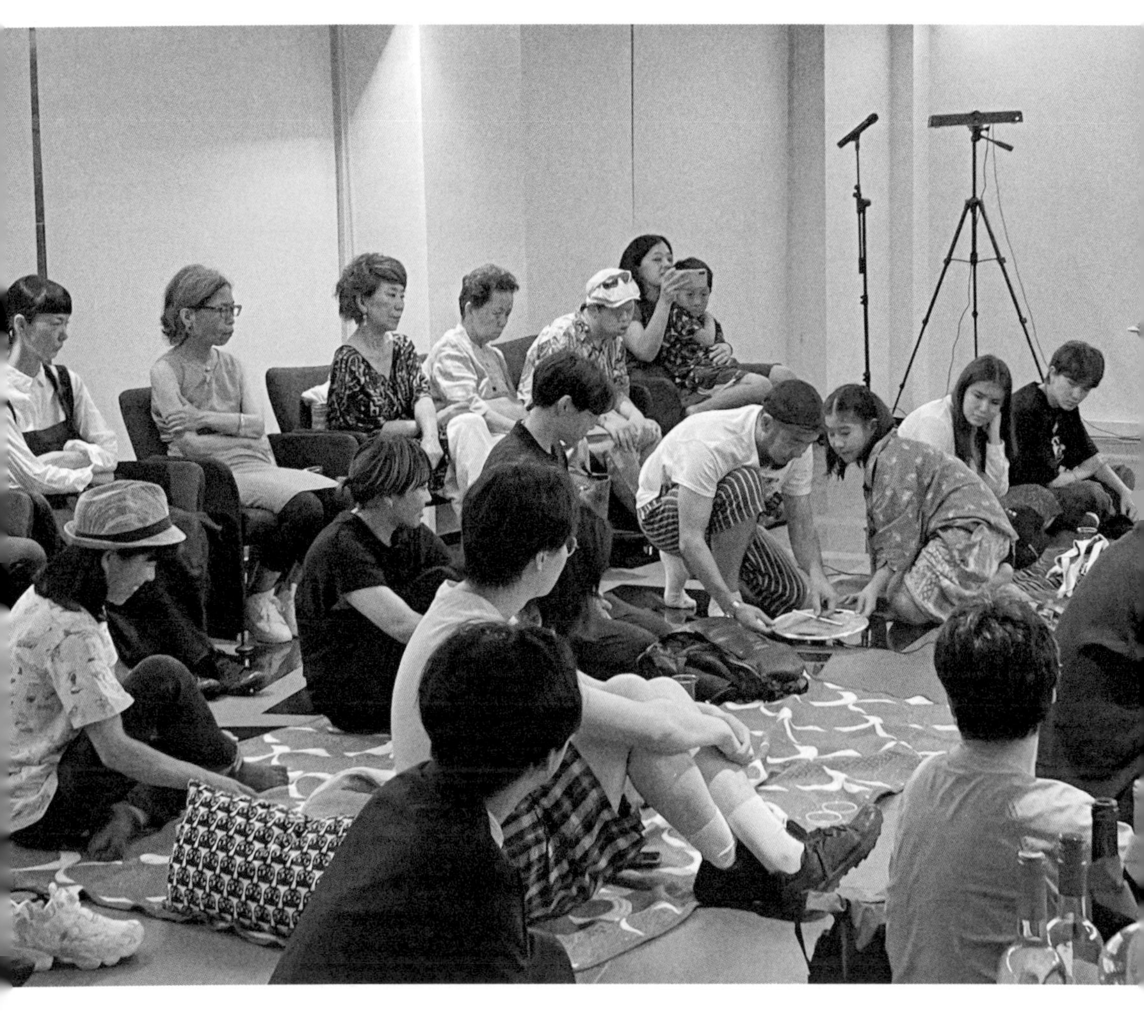

Acoustic Abolitionism: Interview with Wanda Canton

BRANDON LABELLE: We've had the opportunity to welcome you to a number of editions of The Listening Academy, the first in London in August 2022, and then again in October 2022 in Bergen, Norway. Your work on sound and social justice is inspiring, and I'm honored to be able to open this space for dialoguing with you. To begin I wonder if you might briefly introduce yourself and your areas of research – what are you focusing on and in what ways does listening feature?

WANDA CANTON: Thank you for your kind words, it has been great to be involved with The Listening Academy. I've left events feeling so rejuvenated and stimulated, for which I'm very grateful. I'm not sure I can introduce myself as any one "ist": criminologist, musicologist, nihilist? My early influences were law, politics, and psychoanalysis, and I certainly identify as an abolitionist. That is, since an early age I have been concerned about practices of policing and incarceration. Not just in the context of the criminal justice system but within wider social discourse, including psychiatric or therapeutic practices. It has taken me down different diversions and perspectives, but I would say that is what drives me. I didn't come to thinking about listening until later. My focus has previously been the significance of making music and creative self-expression. As a mental health facilitator and service manager, I was interested in how the arts could diversify therapeutic spaces – for those of us put off or excluded from traditional approaches and services. I had begun to consider the capacity of music, sound, and speech to create emotional and symbolic movement – out of depression for example, but also within physically restrictive spaces like prisons or hospitals. By day I would deliver rap and spoken word therapeutic (non-clinical) sessions, and by night I studied. I began to consider that such mediums may be liberating because somebody is *listening*. So I have since turned my attention to the politics of listening; not only how these currently inform policing practices, but whether listening provides opportunities for new social identifications. At least to imagine what they (we) could be.

BRANDON: I appreciate you sharing a bit about your background, and I can see how it's hard to pin down a single position – already you open up a lot of interesting perspectives, and I'm intrigued by how you're working across different sites, discourses and practices. I can imagine moving across academic experience and facilitation work must ground your research and practice, and I read this in your writings and articles, and in the urgency these carry. I want to ask you more about your concern with practices of policing and incarceration, and in what ways sound and music are positioned as carriers of movement or liberation – this finds expression in your project *Sonic Rebellions*. Can you say something about the project, and the relation between sound and social justice?

WANDA: Ironically, given my interest in psychoanalysis, I'm influenced by my family and childhood(!) I came to abolitionism through anti-psychiatric and service-user movements. This has affected me and my family so I was aware of forms of incarceration from quite a young age. I remember feeling quite distressed and alarmed by the practice of imprisonment but without necessarily having the tools to articulate that. Perhaps I was beginning to compare what I knew and experienced to typically one-dimensional representations of people and their complexities, and to see their shortcomings. Meanwhile, both my parents were active in supporting the miners' strike in the Northeast of England; my father was a unionist, and my mother (a saxophonist) was involved in brass bands in Newcastle utilizing music as an expression of solidarity. Politics and music were certainly a big part of our everyday life and often intertwined.

The element of movement appears at the intersection of all these things. There is something optimistic, or imaginative, in the revolutionary marching band and the creation of sound and art from the most confined of spaces. Such confinement can be both physical and internal; I'm tempted to say spiritual to encompass introspection beyond the discourse of mental health, though I have some hesitance using this term. Freud referred to the dream and Lévi-Strauss to the myth as transcending empirical or practical limits. This may be applicable to any creative medium which essentially provides a holding frame within which new possibilities and social relations can be explored. I became interested in rap music particularly, as combining the improvisation and sensory use of rhythm, with the subjectivizing use of speech. Through my facilitation work, I had seen the effects of rhythmic and poetic writing to support people who perhaps felt stuck; in mood, in thought, or in the expectations of self and others; to branch beyond that. For example, using character work and third person pronouns as a way to experience another "role" or expression. I had also become interested in Lacan and signification, noting the therapeutic properties of lyric writing as a way to diversify one's traumatic associations. That is, lyrics can support us to both identify recurring themes or patterns, and to practice widening their frames of reference. To this degree, we can explore and create new linguistic chains and associative memories, which have the potential to "move" us away from traumatic or distressing fixations.

This became the muse for my doctorate; to better understand the transformative attributes of rap music and to learn from rap not only as an epistemic form but as a forum or vehicle within which conversations are held about social conflict and violence, particularly as perpetrated by the state and its institutions. In other words, what are the radical attributes of rap music and what are the consequences of criminalizing it?

Sonic Rebellions is the culmination of many of these experiences and thoughts. I wanted to interrogate the academic space to play with not only what we discuss within the university, but how. I'm very interested in experiential learning – something I have admired being so present within the Listening Academy – and creative ways of sharing ideas. Katherine McKittrick's incredible work on decoloniality very much inspires my thinking about breaking beyond the written text, and how we feel ideas and knowledge. In 2022 we held the inaugural Sonic Rebellions conference to establish a network of activists, academics, and artists. I designed the conference to encourage workshops and interactive sessions alongside more conventional presentations. The invitation to participants was to question: what is the relationship between sound and social justice? Given the breadth of this, we had practitioners and thinkers discussing a range of artistic mediums including soundwalking, mixtaping, reggae sound-systems, immersive audio installations, theater, and social media, to name a few. It felt like an energizing space thanks to the generosity and sincerity of the participants. We published our inaugural edited collection in April 2024 and shortly after held our second "season" of events across the University of Brighton, the London School of Economics and online.

BRANDON: I think you raise a lot of important questions through the Sonic Rebellions project and gatherings – giving more attention to the relationship between sound and social justice, and facilitating meeting points across activistic, academic and artistic communities, feels extremely urgent and rewarding, in terms of building critical bridges, and also creating more experimental forms of knowledge sharing. Lately I've been reading Tanja Dreher's work on the politics of listening, and one of the things she shares is her own experience in organizing and being part of academic gatherings in which the question of privilege has been raised, particularly in terms of *who speaks and who is absent,* what languages are assumed and given value, and in what ways the "good intentions" on the part of organizing cross-cultural discussions can inadvertently perpetuate certain power relations. These are really difficult questions, which are deeply helpful to consider in the work we're doing and in the kind of listening we may want to engage in. I would be interested to hear how you work through your own positionality – or the issue of privilege in general – when it comes to bringing people together, especially to engage with the tough topics such as social conflict? I'm also thinking about how we can negotiate embedded structures of violence that are often present in the room – or how to nurture ways of listening that acknowledge such things?

WANDA: Initially, this concerns the constraint and dictating of knowledge. Assumptions made about language and epistemic spaces may indeed privilege some over others, such as the English language and the university as key sites within which knowledge is shared. However, the rhetoric of privilege increasingly suggests that power and possibility is something that is possessed or owned: a group or individual has or does not have privilege. Whilst it is true that particular material or cultural resources are or are not available to some over others, Foucault's interrogation of power reminds us that power itself is not something retained by any one institution or class; rather it is the dispersal of power that makes it so pervasive and entrenched. The signifiers of power should not be taken to be the problem itself. For example, money, work, housing, respect are only privileges because they are not equally enjoyed; but these things themselves are not privileges, they are basic necessities to quality of life. Power by default constantly strives to diversify its signifiers, attaching importance and meaning to changing units of value – this is how power manifests in multiple social relations and fields. It therefore exists long before and after any given event. My concern is that some attempts to deconstruct power may focus predominantly on individual capital and momentary interventions. The problem with this is that it veers towards a concept of power which is identifiable and deliberate. This suggests that change can be demanded and attained by an individual or collective whilst simultaneously escaping complicity in power relations themselves. This contradicts the ubiquity of power.

An example is the concept of safe spaces often referred to in activist circles. Isn't the fundamental issue that there *is no safe space*? To suggest otherwise sanctifies its facilitators as though they were beyond the myriad of power that makes people and environments unsafe; the difficulty of tackling racism and misogyny for example, is that these are often not consciously developed and become naturalized. We must be cautious not to endow individuals as inherently safe because they possess The Knowledge required to transcend the pervasions of power. Therefore, they are perceived as possessing something of epistemic value over their recipients. Which suggests they can or should impart this knowledge. What distinguishes them from the earlier gatekeepers of knowledge? Is this merely a question of resignification or has the function and operation of power been transformed?

This is particularly problematic for abolitionism if it consolidates the idea that power and violence are deliberately and consciously orchestrated by bad, ignorant, or careless individuals. Sometimes these individuals are censored or removed from spaces, symbolically or directly. Perhaps you can see what I'm getting at here – binaries of people as good/bad and deserving of inclusion/exclusion falls close to logics of policing and incarceration. We must consider whether we can address exclusions without enforcing new ones. It is not my intention to defend relations as they currently are. Rather, my critique is of carceral logic; the attitudes and beliefs that make *policing* inevitable or natural, and the discourse of rights and identity which produce laws and limits to police. To *abolish* and not reform.

I think of my positionality as an ongoing navigation which renders me constantly complicit and subject to power relations. This includes continually discovering what I do not know, what assumptions I make without even realizing it. This must be collaborative and confrontational to some degree (which need not be contradictions), as I would otherwise remain unaware. It is something that can never be fully complete; it is an infinite process. Katherine

McKittrick's work inspires me a lot: the embracing and tolerance of uncertainty and mistakes. I feel like this sentiment could avoid some of the reproductions of power by building solidarity on a shared unknown rather than battle of knowledge.

In the context of *Sonic Rebellions*, I have been conscious of events running primarily within university spaces which I am aware can be intimidating or simply dull to some people. It can be perceived as a problematic institution which is self-superior and hegemonic. However, to completely withdraw from these spaces might only serve the interests of academic elites who would no longer be confronted. Part of my initial motivation was indeed to challenge what topics are discussed within the university and by who. At the 2022 conference there was feedback from some participants that they felt this was a valuable intervention in itself; to be present within the university and to utilize its resources to discuss and present ideas on our own terms. Although we always ensure there is an off-campus, local community collaboration in some way, this is one aspect I would be keen to develop further. It is certainly something we are actively discussing.

BRANDON: I'd like to come back to your work in abolitionism, and the criminalization of rap, which is a focus in your doctoral research as well. In some of your recent writings, you pose the concept of "acoustic abolitionism" and how incarceration works at policing the threat of "noise." How did you arrive at this concept? And how do you see acoustic abolitionism being applied?

WANDA: To try to answer this succinctly, I will accept abolitionism broadly as a starting point. However, it should be acknowledged that abolitionism is not homogeneous, each school of abolitionism champions a specific and localized praxis. American prison-industrial complex abolitionism (PIC) has a different context and may use different strategies to Italian psychiatric abolitionism, for example. Further, we must keep in mind that abolitionism is not yet a commonly accepted position, including among people affected by the criminal justice system. In fact, to return to your earlier question of positionality and power we ought to consider whether we veer towards a vanguardist attitude if we fail to acknowledge the perspectives we disagree with, which may nevertheless come from criminalized communities. The pretence of consensus may not only prevent us from challenging carceral logic (which, by design, is pervasive and self-reproducing), but might inadvertently consolidate dismissive and infantilizing tropes that police and marginalize these same groups as delinquent and ignorant.

On that note, socio-cultural policing is really what I am grappling with. Although abolitionism is most known for its stance against prisons and the institution of the police, it is more broadly concerned with the infrastructure and ideologies which render these a necessity. These ideologies are not necessarily conscious doctrines nor the possession of any one group, but speech, behavior, and relations that organize society. In other words, the *complex* of carceral practices, hence PIC terminology. I think the criminalization of rap music is a good example of this. It's happening right now, with real consequences for individuals and communities so there is an urgency to address this injustice. Rap lyrics have been used in criminal trials since the 90s, and Drill music in the UK is increasingly presented as evidence by prosecution counsel and subject to criminal orders. But rap music has historically been ostracized well beyond the court and continues to be so. Early hip hop was banned from vendor stock, contemporary rap is often banned from social media platforms. Where rap is associated with violence and crime, local communities, parents, and schools are expected to play a preventative or even incapacitating role. Rap is policed well beyond the actual institution of the police. The music itself is increasingly seen as criminal, rather than focusing on demonstrable crimes. For example, there have been injunctions and custodial sentences given for the performance of music – no other crime has alleged. As you raised earlier, we need consider who is absent or prevented from expression. In this case, it is rappers who are predominantly young, Black men. The restriction of movement, expression, and even dress is a form of violence, and it contributes to aggressive tropes of racialized people by reinforcing racist attitudes that people of color are dangerous and need to be controlled. The manifestations of these stereotypes can be deadly, as the Black Lives Movement has highlighted, and as criminalized communities have always called attention to.

If it's helpful, we could think of this as an acoustic version of biopolitics – or as you have better framed it in your own work, acoustic architectures. That is, the way society and power relations are organized around acoustic politics or resources. Jacques Attali explains that sound which disturbs is experienced as noise. Crucially, he says that listening to noise is like being killed. I interpret that murderous quality as a form of conflict; that the noise threatens one's sense of integrity or understanding of the world. For example, rap music has always provided critical commentary on police, racism, and class. It is somewhat of a cultural meme to dismiss contemporary music and its subcultures, including rap, by literally calling it noise. But I also think that *making noise of other people* is a killing of sorts, that rubbishes and makes nonsense their own expression. I'm thinking here of Frantz Fanon's racialized subject who is burst apart by speech which makes Blackness abnormal, out of place, noise. Incarceration, which suppresses all expression, is a form of social death, where people are literally and symbolically silenced. Recently, a service for prisoners that I have worked with has been forced to anonymize prisoners' artwork. Although this could be argued on the grounds of privacy, it seems to be a reaction to public outrage that prisoners should have artistic outlets or expression. It is another example of artistic licence being denied criminalized and racialized groups, and how silencing is a specific form of punishment (again something to be conscious of as we strive for change).

I am exploring whether acoustic abolitionism could be a framework with which to develop an interpretation of how society is policed through sound but consequently, what methods of *sonic rebellions* are resisting. Given the interplaying of these different projects and ideas, I'm still enjoying the opportunity to try to make sense of the links and overlap between power, sound, resistance.

BRANDON: The concept of acoustic abolitionism does open an important discussion, to think further about policing through sound, and how noise can be used to demonize others. Articulating this as an acoustic version of biopolitics is extremely useful – I've been thinking around similar concerns, though more in relation to Deaf culture and how the hearing world has continually subjected the d/Deaf to forms of colonization (something many Deaf scholars have detailed). Following these concerns and arguments, I'm interested to come back to the topic of listening. How does listening operate or contribute to conceptualizing or manifesting social justice – can listening enact a form of sonic rebellion? Do you see political power in listening?

WANDA: This is a question I am thinking through but find myself in knots. Certainly listening features as a political action itself; such as a gesture of allyship, to listen to experiences outside of one's own, whilst it is also a specific punishment; to de-platform public figures following controversy for example and indeed, the censorship of rap music. Listening then, or being listened to, seems to be part of being a citizen/recognizable subject. I am not sure it is so simple, and I will return to this, but as a starting point, via Barthes, we might define hearing as a physiological act, and listening as a psycho-social one. Therefore, the difference between hearing and listening is interpreting meaning. From a structuralist account this is quite literal; the interpretation of signifiers which can be ordered in a multitude of ways, whilst poststructuralist accounts may call attention to what is precluded, or what discursive mechanisms are at play. This suggests that meaning primarily functions at a linguistic, human/living level. That's not to say that an alarm, which is not human, has no meaning – of course it does, and its purpose is to provoke a specific reaction upon hearing it. But there is perhaps not such a fundamental question of subjectivity as there is in listening.

In order to make sense (meaning) of what I listen to, I need to draw conclusions, or assumptions at least, of the subject making the sound and my position in relation to them. This might be a second distinction between hearing/listening. Discussions and theories of recognition have reflected on the element of exchange in addressing another; that subjectivity is implied when being addressed; to listen implies there is a subject to listen to. Hence the importance of listening as a form of solidarity and social accountability which validates and recognizes a speaking subject. Frequently, and particularly in moments of confrontation, one subject asserts their perception to the other and presents it as true. *This is who I am, and this is who you are.* The respondent similarly declares, *yes/no, this is who I am, and this is who you are.* There is less negotiation, perhaps no consideration of how the two entwine, rather an exchange of perceptions.

Listening itself is not necessarily radical; but the negotiation of meaning can be. Jessica Benjamin's concept of Thirding explores the way in which mutually transformative and creative spaces can be created, within which subjects strive not simply to make statements but to ask questions; as posed by Judith Butler and Adriana Cavarero: *who am I? who are you?* And crucially *– who am I in relation to you?* As you have identified, people listen and hear differently, but if it is the introspection and negotiation of subjectivity that is key, listening physically is one mode of politics, but not the only form. The politically transformative potential is not in the affirmation of subjectivity, but in curiosity and fluidity.

Finding this collaborative and creative space is difficult however and questioning the certainty of how we "know" ourselves is painful, as psychoanalysis postulates. Reckoning with the limitations of our own sense of mastery and integrity can feel threatening. It seems that too rigid a desire for knowledge is a hindrance to radical practices of listening which, by involving or acknowledging something outside or beyond the individual subject by default involves an element of uncertainty; how can I relinquish some control, singularity or self-sovereignty to listen without losing myself entirely? I suggest that music is a particularly apt medium to practice these negotiations; as it simultaneously provides opportunities to play and imagine, but within loose boundaries or expectations of composition and form which provide a relative sense of safety and imagination. Concepts and methods articulated in theories of decoloniality might be useful here; articulated by McKittrick, who I have already mentioned, as feeling through text and diversifying the way in which lived experience is known, shared and heard (or more precisely, listened to).

Most interestingly, decoloniality does not focus on language, which is prioritized by structuralist thinking. It is not only the lyrics that move us in a song, but its bassline, composition, and rhythm which provokes emotion and meaning. Existentially, this calls into question the very binary I initially introduced; that of hearing and listening as denoting meaning based on speech/language. What happens, for example, when that alarm I mentioned earlier, goes off at an unexpected time? Or if the context changes? Is this not the deconstructive quality of art; to recontextualize and disturb existing expectations?

Sonic Rebellions, for example, does not simply query the relationship between *language* and social justice, but *sound*. And listening is part of that. I wonder whether an element of the political agency of sound and music is the collaborative nature of listening; the call and response, as reggae and soundsystem studies and practitioners have discussed. However, I would be reluctant to limit the scope here, as I think there is something *empowering* (and I am deliberately avoiding using the word "powerful" for its *power-full* capacities) about creating and sound-making as a solo introspection which is not dependent on an audience. Perhaps then, there is as much of an individual imperative and practice of listening as a social one. There is a further question underlying that I grapple with, and that is of agency/passivity. Is it sufficient to passively listen; to hear without action? Arguably, *not* acting has political repercussions where it facilitates space for other forms of agents or subjectivity to emerge. I wonder whether listening is realized as a political act because it provokes movement, but not necessarily of the listener. And it cannot be limited to language as neither the material nor the response are necessarily linguistic. Perhaps political visibility cannot be encompassed by the speaking subject, but rather, the listened-to subject. However, as Dylan Robinson articulates in his critique of "hungry listening," it is not simply enough to situate listening as between a listener and listened-to subject, but how these very subjectivities are intertwined and assumed.

HENRY IVRY

Listening to Infrastructure: Acoustic Circulation & Black Resistance

I.

We live in a moment of infrastructural crisis. Decades of privatization, so the commonsense narrative goes, means that the large-scale systems of circulation that we often take for granted – from waterworks to highways to data clouds – have begun to collapse with an increasing frequency and amplification in the contemporary. Literary scholar Dominic Davies offers a helpful periodization from the post-War period to the present that traces the growth of the usage of the term infrastructure as an index of the exponential acuteness of this crisis.

He writes, "The increase in the usage of the word 'infrastructure,' itself tracks this shift from public to private interests" (2023, p. 37). As the nation-state begins to fray, Davies contends, so too do the infrastructural systems that once sustained and supported the projects of those nation-states.[1] There has been a perceptual amplification of the infrastructures that surround us thanks to the increasing interrelated and ambient crises of geopolitics, economics, ecology, and racialization. As cultural theorist Lauren Berlant argued, the contemporary is "a scene shaped by the infrastructural breakdown of modernist practices of resource distribution, social relation, and affective continuity" (2016, p. 394). It's no wonder that questions of infrastructure inundate everything from RSS feeds to the policy platforms of most political parties across the globe. Infrastructure is both the solution and the problem: it is weaponized for insidious economic and geopolitical aims and/or touted as solution to entrenched social, political, or climatic issues.

Without trying to gloss over the very real ways in which we do live in a contemporary of infrastructural crisis, this isn't the whole story. There is an ahistorical risk to think that it's only now we've noticed the "boring things" that surround us (1999, p. 377). The Marshall Plan, after all, was specifically conditioned by infrastructure, as was decolonization, to name just two examples.[2] What has changed, I want to argue, isn't that we've finally begun to realize that infrastructures are crumbling and/or complicit in the maintenance of a violent colonial modernity, but rather our relationship to those infrastructures has changed. Or, if not *changed* per se, we've noticed those relationships in different ways. And, as I argue below, what has begun to emerge are new ways of listening to infrastructure, tuning to unexpected frequencies as a way to both navigate and resist the large-scale systems of circulation that we are enmeshed in.

What is also important about our contemporary moment is that concomitant with a newborn hyperawareness of infrastructure, infrastructure has also become both the means and form of contemporary politics. This is to say that the epoch of imagining infrastructure as the supposed neutral arbiter of circulation and flow is no longer a tenable fantasy (if it ever was). From Gaza to

Kyiv, from the extraction of cobalt to AI prompt engineers, infrastructure has become, as communications scholar Darrin Barney describes it, its own "form of politics" (2022, p. 226). This marks a scalar shift in contemporary politics. Questions of citizenship and national sovereignty are subsumed and usurped by the infrastructural, as politics becomes, following Judith Butler, about the building, maintenance, and contestation over "a certain kind of inhabitable ground" (2016, p. 14).

An infrastructural shift in the constitution and maintenance of the polity begs a question: how do we approach politics when politics is infrastructural? Two decades ago, when there were the first murmurings of infrastructure as a site worthy of analysis within the academe, infrastructural critique was focused on an economy of identification, making visible the salient operations and subtending logics of capital and colonial violence routed and circulated (and occasionally interrupted) through infrastructure. This was the emergence of what sociologist Susan Leigh Star and informatics scholar Geoffrey Bowker in *Sorting Things Out* (2000) called *inversion* where background and foreground were refigured. In the interceding decades, it's become clear that this doesn't go far enough. In a pointed critique against visibility as a means of galvanizing political action, comparative literature scholar Jennifer Wenzel argues that there is a dogmatic "assumption that seeing is *knowing* and that *knowing* is a catalyst for *caring, acknowledging,* or *acting* to rectify suffering or injustice" (2019, p. 14). She continues by stating that, if we've learned anything from the past decade and change of the failure of transnational climate action, it's that seeing isn't ever enough. To stretch this further, seeing itself has been the dominant sensory technology through which infrastructure has been constituted, another iteration of what Ronald Radano and Tejumola Olaniyan name an "occularcentric" mode of knowledge creation emblematic of empire (2016, p. 2). In short, this critical economy of visibility limits the ways in which we might engage with infrastructures to start rebuilding the world differently. As Berlant writes, "Infrastructure is not identical to system or structure, as we currently see them, because infrastructure is defined by the movement or patterning of social form. It is the living mediation of what organizes life: the lifeworld of structure" (2016, p. 393). What Berlant points to is the fact that relying on sight means we often misrecognize infrastructure as structure – mistaking volatility and malleability with static and intractable monoliths. So how might we engage differently with infrastructure? Is there another sensory encounter that might help facilitate the fostering and cultivation of alternate relations and politics?

II.

What I want to do in this essay, then, is think about another way of relating to infrastructure and infrastructural politics, by setting aside the eye/I of modernity and tuning to the acoustic. In *Making Peace with Nature* (2022), anthropologist Eleanna J. Kim coins what she calls *rogue infrastructures* to trace the different constellations of human-nonhuman entities she encounters in the Korean Demilitarized Zone that runs along the 38th Parallel in Korea. She locates:

> [Alternative] infrastructures in that they are human-nonhuman-technical networks that exist in relation to the infrastructure of division, while generating other flows, circulations, and temporalities. These flows, circulations, and temporalities, in turn, often exceed the material and imaginative bounds of capitalist logics, sovereign power, ethnonationalist teleologies, and anthropocentric metaphysics. (2022, pp. 26 – 27)

Reading this description of rogue infrastructure, I was reminded of another "human-nonhuman-technical network" that both works through existing flows and circulations while also creating its own mode of disruption, *sound*. Following Kim's capacious definition of infrastructure (though it's worth adding that infrastructure is, definitionally, capacious), I wonder how we might listen to infrastructure? And, just as importantly, can we hear within infrastructure the possibilities of a world outside of its inherited logic of racial capitalism and colonial dispossession?

In posing these questions, I'm struck by how sound is so often held at arm's distance from infrastructural studies. This feels counterintuitive. Consider a passage from the work of Jennifer Hsieh's research on noise pollution in Taiwan where she describes walking through Taipei at night:

> Other machines, like air conditioners, water cooling towers, and generators, were common items [...] Forging a relation between human life and economic production, the sounds of industrial and commercial life were, and continue to be, the sounds of the neighborhood. Moreover, mysterious humming and clocking, the buzzing of electricity lines, the howling sound of wind blowing against urban structures ... reconstitute the meaning of environmental noise. (2021, p. 494)

What Hsieh is describing is the fact that the acoustic constitutes much of our phenomenological experience of the infrastructures that surround us – from the rumble of air conditioners to the ambient hum of electricity. But still, there is something of a critical impasse when it comes to thinking of the aural in infrastructural terms. What we are often left with, as Andy Stuhl argues, is a rendering of sound articulated as "an infrastructural effect, not as a material event capable of producing infrastructure in its own right" (2021, p. 273). But, as Stuhl and others have suggested, there is a lot of work to be done if we take seriously the idea that infrastructure and sound are co-constitutional – structuring and restructuring one another.

In *Audible Infrastructures: Music, Sound, Media* (2021) this question and its modalities are explored by thinking about infrastructure through the acoustic. As social anthropologist Penny Harvey puts it, "The questions of what it takes to produce and to circulate music (in other words to attend to *the infrastructures of music*) and what such circulations in turn produce (in other words to attend to *music as infrastructure*)" (2021, p. 62). What Harvey is describing is how sound and music are both contingent upon infrastructure relations, but also – and this is what interests me – how sound becomes infrastructural in enabling and disabling certain flows and patterns. Take, for example, the work of the Sonic Research Insurgency Group, a collective of Chicago academics, activists, and artists exploring the politics of sound. On the one hand, they explore how sound can constitute an environment of oppression and an extension of state violence. They write:

> Sirens ring out; helicopters whir; police amplify their commands; they blast their long-range acoustic devices and set up their gunshot detection technologies. What we hear, mis-hear, do not hear, cannot hear, or choose not to hear plays an integral role in the structuring of social and political life, particularly when what constitutes sound and noise are leveraged in the struggle over social power and public space. (2021, n.p.)

The Sonic Research Insurgency Group is describing, in part, the work done by Medium and Long-Range Acoustic Devices (MRAD and LRADs). Using sound, these weapons are designed to impair and hinder the circulation of specific sounds in place of others, particularly by overlapping with the range of human speech. These weapons have been a staple of policing tactics since they were first used in the early 2000s.

At the same time, though, the Sonic Research Insurgency Group, also figures alternate ways to inhabit the world through the acoustic. In this same essay, they point to the possibility of an otherwise world that can emerge by retuning to alternate tones and timbres: "Social groups are produced and produce themselves through their listening practices and shared repertoires of sounding out, even as they struggle against the weaponization of sound and dominant society's authority over acceptable aural ways of being" (2021, n.p.). Although they don't use the term *infrastructure*, what the Sonic Research Insurgency Group is describing is indeed a sonic infrastructure that is at once constituted through racialized oppression and white supremacy, but also one that contains the possibilities for insurgency. This is about looking for ways to begin enabling and patterning new socialities through acoustic cohabitation and intimacy.

III.

My own research on Black culture, aesthetics, and politics, has long been struck by the alternative lifeworlds and possibilities that are opened up through Black sound. From the ineffable violence of Aunt Hester's scream to the insurgent sites of knowledge that hover on the edge of the plantation, Black sound has long been a repository of the violence of infrastructures while pointing to alternate frequencies that aren't exhausted by those white supremacist systems of circulation. If what we are looking for are alternative ways of inhabiting and co-opting existent infrastructure, exceeding to echo Eleanna J. Kim, "the material and imaginative bounds of capitalist logics, sovereign power, ethnonationalist teleologies, and anthropocentric metaphysics" (2022, p. 26), my goal here is to begin to listen to Black sound as one such site of alternative infrastructural possibility. To make this claim is to begin listening to an inchoate vibrational wave in contemporary Black sound studies that explores how sound is instrumental in building and rebuilding our world. In the work of DJ, interdisciplinary artist and theorist Tao Leigh Goffe, she explores how the development of sound system technology and culture in Jamaica both produced new technologies and communities and inhabited old forms of infrastructure by enacting "sonic cosmologies or ritual worlds [that] offer makeshift spaces of do-it-yourself desire" (2020, p. 104). Likewise, media culture theorist Andrew Navin Brooks' research on *fugitive listening* uses the acoustic as a way to understand the politics of the riot via "a noise that contains multiple centers, a polyphonic enunciation that cannot be contained or captured, a sonicity of continuous discontinuity that suggests the possibility of a reconfiguration of relations" (2023, p. 3). Although infrastructure is again not named here, both Goffe and Brooks point to how infrastructure and the acoustic converge via Black sound. Said differently, these are descriptions of the ways that Black sound both constitutes and is constituted through infrastructure. The music and sounds that these theorists are tracing are composed through "human-nonhuman-technical networks" that open into new ontological and epistemological possibilities. It's easy to look at the history of Black music to think of clear iterations of this insurgent infrastructure – from dub technicians rewiring their machines to early acid house producers reinventing the Roland TB – 30; from the infinite half-life of the "Amen Break" to Pirate Radio stations. It's impossible to read the history of Black sound, in other words, without thinking about its simultaneously recursive and discursive relationship to its infrastructural conditions of production and otherwise possibilities of short-circuiting those same conditions.

But what does this actually sound like? Anything like an exhaustive inventory of these acoustics wouldn't be possible, but I want to conclude by listening to a record that gestures towards the insurgent possibilities of Black sonic infrastructures. Emeka Ogboh's 2021 EP, *Beyond The Yellow Haze*, is a short record built through an infrastructural logic. Pieced together from field recordings of infrastructure – traffic jams, markets, and brothels from his home in Lagos, Nigeria – Ogboh looks for different ways to use these sounds. These infrastructural sites signal for Ogboh both the residue and hangover of a colonial infrastructural system, but also form the sonic palette for him to begin creating new Black lifeworlds. There is a dual logic at work here. On the one hand, there is an acoustic amplification of the petromodernity infrastructures that continue to extract from Nigeria (not to mention other postcolonial spaces globally). We can hear this in the sense of immanent dread in the dub-soaked caverns of empty space on opener "Lekki Aiah Freeway." Likewise, there is something spectral about the descending minor chords that warp and warble over the pattering rain and dying honks of cars on "Palm Groove." But Ogboh also sees ways to reinhabit and reimagine these infrastructural sites that are so complicit in maintaining colonialism's logistical wake. The rhythms that underpin this haunted extractivist economy are made nimble, almost gossamer-like, as Ogboh creates miniature latticework drum patterns that shape-shift ever so slightly. On "Danfo Mellow," a faint xylophone-like melody plonks across the top while freeway chatter is refitted into a dulled melodic effect over a minimal techno loop.

Things get even brighter on album centerpiece "Everydaywehustlin." The name itself is a condensed meme of neoliberal culture, a phrase that crystallizes the globalization of precarity and its exportation. The hustle culture of B-Boys and early American hip-hop apotheosizing into Rick Ross's lyrics before becoming transformed into gentrified millennial soundbites and then moving back across the Atlantic and becoming engrained in the post-colonial post-socialist Nigerian imaginary. This system of circulation that is embedded within the track's name – a strange infrastructural metonymy – is inverted by the way the track actually functions by reversing the logic of infrastructural policing. Ogboh begins the song from the site of individuation as he expands the track's aperture to bring the gradual collectivization of voices into focus. The individual voices of what are presumed to be market sellers and passing traffic are gathered together against the heavily processed synthesizer stabs and the skittish four-four kick drum pattern that emerges underneath along the sulking pulses of sub bass. The component parts are both greater than and less than the sum of what emerges. This is not the killing rhythm of a colonial infrastructure, but rather an insurgent groove of Black life as it is imagined coming together. In this way, I see a resonance with how Black and religious studies scholar Ashon T. Crawley describes Black singing as a moment of entanglement within "an ongoing collaboration, the collaboration fundamental to alternate modalities of existence" (2020, p. 122). And the track itself – with its mixture of organic and synthetic samples, its vivid sense of livingness contrasted with the mechanical austerity of its techno rhythms – does not try to resolve the paradox at play. Instead, Ogboh positions the onus back on us, requiring his audience to listen to the music differently, to try and get outside the locked groove of infrastructural extraction into some larger, messier, and funkier types of entanglements.

If infrastructure names the forming of social patterns, then there is something very pointed about the ways that these tracks are instrumental in converging around danceable rhythms and grooves. This is, I should emphasize, a funky record from start to finish. Almost any one of these tracks would keep a late-night dance floor grooving with their respective low-end heft. This is, for my money anyways, how Ogboh narrates the possibility of a future collectivization that emerges with and through sonic infrastructures. Working with the infrastructural building blocks of anti-Black violence, Ogboh builds a rhythm and a beat that is danceable – sub bass pulses that reach deep into the body while the field recordings dart in and out of the slippery wobbles of the hand percussion. What we hear here is a funk that Black and queer studies theorist Rinaldo Walcott might describe as a "a call to some kind of action" (2021, p. 69). For Walcott, funk names not just an aesthetic, but a political form, a way of thinking through a radical Black freedom that isn't tethered to the matrices of coloniality. As the record forms, disintegrates, and reforms into tracks that have the trappings of techno, there is a bricolage of funkiness that is demonstrative of a "sense of autonomy and self-creation beyond the imposed scripts of death demonstrated in its multiple expressive modes of forms of Black life beyond white supremacist logics" (2021, p. 71). Finding moments to dance, provisional and ephemeral rhythms from within these infrastructures is a way of arguing that funkiness is a necessary antidote to the "white supremacist logics" from which it is assembled.

The rhythm that emerges in "Everydaywehustlin" is similar to the one that underpins the work of urbanist AbdouMaliq Simone. Simone is interested in the acoustics of infrastructure and the way they facilitate the logistical circulations of global white supremacy. But he also sees infrastructures as opening alternative rhythms. He writes:

> [Infrastructures] are not matters of 'spontaneous flow' but of calibration and measure [...] Measures consist of many devices, ways of seeing, and calculating, many operating according to a 'strange' mathematics. Rhythm is produced from these measures, from the efforts of the connected and disconnected to create refrains, momentary stabilities that offer up a repertoire of vernaculars, gestures, and sensibilities that can be then taken up to twist and turn a place into some malleable yet steady arena for people to pay attention to each other, engage each other, or not (2022, p. 17).

For him, a way of reinhabiting infrastructure is through the creation of new and different types of rhythm. Simone turns to the improvisational work of the Art

Ensemble of Chicago to demonstrate this, describing their occasionally cacophonous, polyrhythmic music as "infrastructures for the enunciation of the exaltation required for collaborative practices – the sense of wonderment and ease required to live-with the ebbs and flows, the constraints and traumas of everyday life" (2022, p. 20). What he is describing here is an insurgent sense of non-teleological circulation, a patterning that doesn't quite reproduce. The goal is not to merely try to maintain the circulatory rhythms of an infrastructure as such. Instead, the aim is to embrace the polyphonous cacophony that exists within any infrastructure that itself can open into the otherwise possibilities of Black infrastructures. This is where I see the possibility of Black resistance emerging through the acoustic. This is a type of sonic infrastructure that follows Black studies scholar Katherine McKittrick in trying to "[groove] out of the logics of racism and into black life" (2021, p. 164). Groove and funk are, to my ears, the register at which the acoustic remains rich in timbres of both ecological and anti-state possibilities, a repository for a new set of sonorous freedoms that do not simply refuse the syncopations of state violence but affirms, announces, and amplifies riotous modes of living.

NOTES

1. As comparative literary scholar Brian Whitener writes: "It is hard to imagine turning to the state in the present – where there once might have been points of entry for negotiation, cooptation, and mediation, today one more often finds doors leading into the carceral, judicial, and deportation systems or into necropolitical futures" (2020, n.p.)

2. We need only think of Frantz Fanon's introductory chapter to *The Wretched of the Earth*, where he details how colonialism is an interface of infrastructural dispossession. Fanon states, "The colonist's sector is a sector built to last, all stone and steel" then adding, "It's a sector of lights and paved roads, where the trash cans constantly overflow with strange and wonderful garbage, undreamed-of leftovers" (2021, 103)

BIBLIOGRAPHY

Barney, D. (2022) "Infrastructure and the Form of Politics," *Canadian Journal of Communications* 46(2) (2022). pp. 225 – 246.

Berlant, L. (2016) "The Commons: Infrastructure for Troubling Times," *Environment and Planning* 34(3), pp. 393 – 419.

Bowker. G, and S. Star (2000) *Sorting Things Out: Classification and Its Consequences*. Boston: Massachusetts Institute of Technology.

Brooks, A. N. (2023) "Anticipation, abolition, possibility: on riots, networked communication, and listening," *Cultural Studies*, 37 (6) pp. 944 – 968.

Butler, J. (2016) "Rethinking Vulnerability and Resistance," *Vulnerability in Resistance*. eds. Judith Butler, Zeynep Gambetti, Leticia Sabsay, Durham: Duke University Press, pp. 12 – 28.

Crawley, A. T. (2020) *The Lonely Letters*. Durham: Duke University Press.

Davies, D. (2023). *Broken Promise of Infrastructure*. London: Lawrence Wishart.

Fanon, F. (2021). *The Wretched of the Earth* 60th Anniversary Edition. trans. Richard Philcox. New York: Grove Atlantic Press.

Goffe, T. L. (2020) "Bigger than the Sound: The Jamaican Chinese Infrastructures of Reggae," *Small Axe* 24(3), pp. 97 – 127.

Harvey, P. (2021) "Making Music, Building Roads: A Reflection on Sound, Materiality, and Social Transformation," *Audible Infrastructures: Music, Sound, Media*. eds. Kyle Devine and Alexandrine Boudreault-Fournier, Oxford: Oxford University Press, pp. 62 – 74.

Hseih, C. J. (2021) "Noise viscerality: navigating relations in a sonic climate," *HAU Journal of Ethnographic Theory* 11(2), pp. 491 – 505.

Kim, J. E. (2022) *Making Peace with Nature: Ecological Encounters Along the Korean DMZ*. Durham: Duke University Press.

McKittrick, Katherine (2021) *Dear Science and Other Stories*. Durham: Duke University Press.

Radano, R. and T. Olaniyan. (2016) "Introduction: Hearing Empire," *Audible Empire: Music, Global Politics, Critique*. eds. Ronald Radano and Tejumola Olaniyan. Durham: Duke pp. 1 – 22.

Simon, A. (2022). *The Surrounds: Urban Life within and beyond Capture*. Durham: Duke University Press.

Sonic Research Insurgency Group. (2021) "Introduction: Conversations on Sound and Power." Available at: https://march.international/introduction-conversations-on-sound-and-power/

Star, S. (1999) "The Ethnography of Infrastructure." *American Behavioral Scientist* 43 (3), pp. 377 – 391.

Stuhl, A. (2021) "Acoustic Infrastructure: The Sounds and Politics of Radio Tests in American Emergency Broadcasting," *Canadian Journal of Communication* 46(2), pp. 271 – 290.

Walcott, R. (2021) *The Long Emancipation: Moving Toward Black Freedom*, Durham: Duke University Press.

Wenzel, J. (2019) *The Disposition of Nature: Environmental Crisis and World Literature*, New York: Fordham Press.

Whitener, B. (2020) "Detroit's Water Wars: Race, Failing Social Reproduction, and Infrastructure," *Comparative Literature and Culture* 22 (2), np.

SARA MIKOLAI

Dance as resonant doing in the myriad of constraints

There is something about stepping into a dark space. It has been explored by a number of artists. Before I did; somewhere across different territories in a concurrent time window of the present; and most likely, many more will continue to explore the body, movement, dance, in darkness. I like these kinds of shared explorations across time, space and context, especially unknowingly. It says something about our shared experience of being alive, of being in these bodies, while at the same time, having innately different experiences in resonance with our surroundings, how and with whom, and under which circumstances we grew up, we live with. How our bodies exist, are perceived by others, by ourselves. How a glance at our bodies makes us feel safe, unsafe, seen, unseen, loved, unloved. A language of the body, a language of the eyes. A simple decision to shift that space of communication, a decision such as switching the light off.

Or not switching it on.

Of placing a few table lands on the floor, in the back of the theater. What is this dance, that can't be seen? I do not aim for absolute certainty here. It is rather a subtle hint, traces of movements, of embodied knowledge, of the question of constraints and freedom and whatever these mean. It is that space of not quite knowing, of questioning how we define things, bodies and ultimately dance, to a definite, where I suggest its intention. It is a proposal to rethink what dance is and how we experience it.

As a Sri Lankan Tamil and diasporic dancer from Berlin, this dance holds a varied significance to our community of refugees and migrants. The high caste and class context of India and its diaspora does not apply to us or to our bodies within our dance community as it does for the dominant dance field in India. However, the histories of marginal communities are intertwined in regards to precolonial, colonial, post- and neocolonial times, and of course the relation between Tamils from the island and Tamils on the mainland as well (this in itself is a complex conversation, and also triggers wounds from the war). My inquiries into this dance arise from the peculiar position of having been passed on the dance along with its classical aesthetics and values, which I critically question, while at the same time never having been in the position of the social status of classical dancers and musicians in South Asia, which have predominantly marginalized the origins of the temple and ritual practice and its communities. Perhaps it is precisely from this ambiguous position of another marginalized dancer from which my solidarity arises, with those whose inheritance and practice were disrupted, and a shared experience of dismissal from these dominant scenes, aesthetics and players – even in the diaspora between the different South Asian communities (which is why Western umbrella diversity politics that ignore local disparities, which play out in the diasporas, can be really difficult to cope with). In my practice, I aim to address this through a long-term commitment to unlearning and fostering a new relationship with the dance that allows space for this critique.

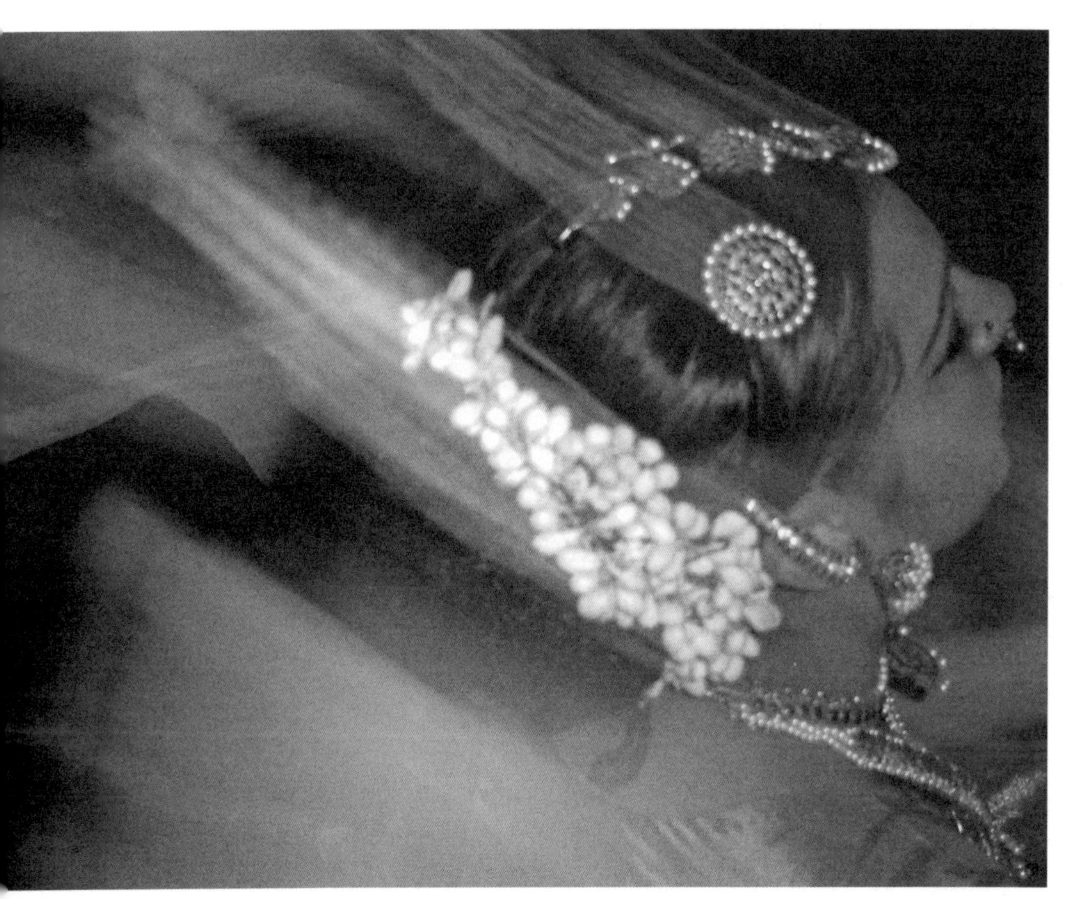

This piece serves as an opening to that dialogue.

to dance without the burden of the gaze, or
to be seen. without the burden of beauty
and perfection. or hastiness.
or show.

                                   to inquire.
to make space for rest, for the subtle,
the sensory. for embodied movement and
passed on knowledge to change the linear
course, to take its own way and explore
space, time and connection.

I don't believe that being seen by the center (and I am leaving it open as to which center, as there are many kinds of it) is always the solution to every critique. In fact, with this piece and practice, I was able to evolve it precisely by stepping away from centralized cultural politics and aesthetics, even during times of diversity politics, particularly from a diasporic perspective that extends beyond the European context. Dramaturgical advice in Western theaters often insists on putting our works only in relation to a Western audience, supposedly as a strategy of empowerment, making visible, and teaching about us, but I find it does the opposite: I find it to be reductive, out of context and flattening. And so I am extremely grateful to those who have provided me the space to share this performance piece for what it truly is, allowing it to exist outside the constraints of a production tailored for success. This piece also critiques this expectation of how we are supposed to convey our dance works in theaters in Europe. This is a crucial aspect of my work, highlighting that Western performing arts aesthetics is its own form of colonizing our practices, which are more rooted in communal and ritual contexts.

And listening proposes precisely this – to be with it, witness, receive, be immersed as a listener, not only

observer.

I so appreciate participating in these gatherings of listening. The shared intentions of listening creates space to witness what lies in the cracks. The absence of spectacle, the invitation to collective listening, and the sharing of our journeys were beautiful moments for me that allowed me to feel acknowledged in the uncertain paths I have taken, while also helping me recognize the trajectory my practice has followed into artistic knowledge production and research.

The presentation at The Listening Academy in Bergen preceded the performance itself. It encompassed my reflections and connections, ranging from historical context to my own current practice. Sometimes, I struggle with what to share. There is so much to convey, and I feel compelled to be transparent about how my reality and work are intertwined with history. How to be precise, without overloading. How I even came to dance this dance today, to my inquiries, of who danced and inquired before me, or at the same time in a different geography with the same dance. Of the ancestral connections. The colonial violence. Nationalist violence. I am not sure how I feel about the presentation itself precisely because of the magnitude of this complexity, which can be paralyzing as a practitioner – where does critical inquiry, reflection, creativity, artistic exploration and proposal meet, where does one weigh more than the other. It is this tightrope of engaging with our *traditions* (a term I engage with critically), histories and connections. But it all also informs one and another, and artistic practice and research emerges in that space. I often insist, as with this performance, to separate the sharing of information and the experience of dance. Because the dance practice, performance situations and aesthetics I intend to share already carry that information. I remember this question arose during the presentation, and I remember it was taken back after the performance. I am happy that witnessing a performance can do that. To allow dance, music, performance to be witnessed without simultaneous explanation. That in itself is a decolonial process.

Because the piece adapts to the space and is so much about what is unspoken between the performer and the audience, it works differently in each space and situation, in each geography. The performance in Bergen was truly special for me. It resonated. Perhaps it is because there is already this invitation to listen, and the sharing of different practices of and angles to listening through the whole program of The Listening Academy. Like I wrote earlier – this shared space of intention makes a difference. When this listening space is already opened up, explored, and shared, undoubtedly the experience of this dance performance is deepened. When it is not only perceived as a confrontation to the gaze, the removal of visual transparency, but as an invitation to be immersed in it through the ear, and hopefully for some the other senses as well: the touch between ones own body and the space, on a chair, floor; the awareness of the others in space is heightened through the lack of a spotlighted protagonist. When smell comes in. When muscle tension is recognized and let go of.

And to witness from here.

I felt the attentiveness and care of the audience. It allowed me to improvise with my ankle bells in new ways.

Posing, exploring and letting go of questions. Acknowledging the connections.

To move between the subtle and quiet.

> And to re-approach what slowness, speed, volume, time and
> timing can do when they are not an aesthetic flaunt.

To practice a connection between movement and sound,
dance and music, as one.

> To explore dance in resonance with space and sound.
> In this doing, I find a lost intention of this dance.

LUÍSA SANTOS

Imagining narratives via care and listening

The journey of the research presented at The Listening Academy, in Bergen, in November 2022, started through an encounter at the *Tate Intensive: Making Tomorrow's Art Museum* at Tate Modern, in London, back in late 2016. In particular, this included addressing the current challenges that creative industries are facing at the levels of gender and racial diversity and the need for greater forms of decolonization on the part of institutions such as the Tate. We met in the new extension of the museum, whose presence has contributed to the gentrification of the local environment, with social and economic consequences for the diversity of people the institution is aiming to represent. There was no in-depth discussion about the types of narratives produced by this diversity of people and if/how these impact on institutional environmental practices. This prompted me to analyze the practices of diverse art institutions across Europe, an analysis which has so far indicated that there is generally a fragmentary project-based approach to connecting environmental and social issues in institutional practices (Santos, 2022a).

Following this initial encounter in 2016, in 2020, participating in the conference "Considering Monoculture" organized by the Museum of Contemporary Art Antwerp, the Van Abbemuseum and the deBuren, an interdisciplinary program considering manifestations of monoculture in art, culture and its institutions, I experienced another encounter, that of radical movements of permaculture, which led me to recognize similarities between agricultural and cultural-(art) institutional relations (Santos and Maurício, 2020). The work that follows is to some degree a response to these two important encounters. Furthermore, it is grounded in a caring ethos, involved with those worried about colonial legacies, anti-ecological times, processes, and agencies. Here, listening emerged as a tool and a place of unsilencing (Santos and Maurício, 2021). If, on the one hand, listening may be overwhelmed with cacophony, and the intensification of noise today, a more attentive ear may discover a range of diverse voices whose silenced narratives carry the potential for social transformation (Santos, 2022a). It is my view that caring for what is heard can lead us to appreciate and even incorporate such narratives, allowing for greater social and environmental understanding (Santos, 2022b).

I'll start with an introduction to the context of the research, in which I'll introduce the problem (or the protagonist, if this is to be heard as a story), and I'll follow with a series of speculative proposals.

CONTEXT

By the mid-20th century, with the aftermath of the second world war, over which time nearly all European colonies gained independence, entering so-called post-colonial and neocolonialist relations, and when unity and the creation of a European identity was understood as essential for the survival of Europe, monocultures appeared as a solution to maximize agricultural production, resulting in vast areas of identical crops. These apparently harmonious monocultures, however, pose "a clear and present threat to biodiversity, sustainable agriculture, and food security" (Grant, 2007). Today, despite the knowledge of the danger of monocultures, and that human diversity and biodiversity are linked (see, i.e., Martin and Persic, 2008), it could be said that many European art institutions and universities mimic monocultures in their research, organizational, and curatorial practices, which are not racially and gender diverse (particularly in higher positions) and harm the environment (via the waste produced, addition of more carbon into the atmosphere with art internationalization and mobility, for example). Western supremacy within art and culture is more than a problem for the arts, it is a problem for the ways we can think about culture as a space of survival, imaginative thinking, and responsibility toward humans and non-human others (Bell, 2022).

Presently, it is imperative to understand the above-described long-standing challenge of art institutions and universities, and the ways in which the issue of monocultures in agriculture can be translatable onto the contexts of art institutions and universities. The main technique in monoculture farming is to replant the same crop species in the same fields, with no other type of plant included. This is the basis of large-scale farm corporations. Reusing the same soil, instead of rotating three or four different crops following a pre-determined cycle, can lead to plant pathogens and diseases. The pathogens adapt to the soil and attack the crops and the quantity produced eventually, and steadily, decreases. Furthermore, using pesticides and herbicides in the same fields can have similar effect, as the soil/flora/fauna adapt to it, thus leading to the need to use stronger types of insect and weed killers. Today, many art institutions and universities' practices can be read as monocultural: the main technique in monoculture institutional practices is to (re)contextualize the same artistic voices and ideas in the same institutional contexts, with no other types of artistic voices and knowledge included. This is the basis of large-scale art institutions and universities. Reusing the exact same voice, instead of rotating three or four different artistic practices following a pre-determined context, can lead to silencing other practices and knowledge(s). The reused voices adapt to the institutional context and attack the other artistic practices and the quality of the critical analysis of the world that they produce eventually decreases. Furthermore, showing the same voices in the same context over and over can have the same effect, as the context (institutions and their audiences) adapts to them, accepting them as the (only) valid knowledge or aesthetic epistemology. Of course, this is a literal adaptation from the agricultural to the artistic field. However, much like the agricultural monocultures, monocultural artistic and institutional practices can be vastly damaging if unchecked.

It is my view that European art institutions and universities are facing two major challenges: to be representative of the human diversity of the world they inhabit; and to decrease the impact their activities have (such as massive international exhibitions and exchange / mobility programs) onto the environmental crisis, which is putting at risk human and more-than-human diversity and survival. Grounded in the recognition of these challenges, in the last decade, European governmental entities have been setting criteria to grant financial support to creative industries, calling for solutions to the lack of racial and gender diversity and representation, and for adopting a greater role in securing a green and sustainable future for Europe. These criteria, however, have mostly failed to link the importance of racial and gender diversity with the call for an environmentally sustainable future. One must ask: what are the links between race, gender, and the environment in today's European art institutions and universities? Despite wide recognition that the environmental crisis has an uneven impact for different genders and races in different parts of the world, and that the legacy of European colonial history is reflected in race, gender, social inequ(al)ities, and in extractive cultures of the environment, existing literature in the creative industries has avoided discussing how multiple intersections of race, gender, and the environment inform / are informed by diverse (post- and de-)colonial experiences of injustice, inequity, and unsustainability in producing, accessing and participating in art and culture. Furthermore, existing literature on the environmental impact of creative industries mostly focuses on the (ab)use of material resources and CO_2 emissions in shipping artworks and in massive international exhibitions, biennials, and exchange / mobility programs without discussing the loss of knowledge and aesthetic epistemologies in monocultural practices in art institutions and universities. In other words, aside from the impact of material activities onto the environment, how does the marginalization of diverse knowledge and aesthetic epistemologies impact on what we know about and how we live with other human and natural forms of life that inhabit our world? While art institutions and universities are fundamental to societal development, the basis of their practices often rely on traditions of a colonial past, which perpetuate grand narratives (told by the elite few who have access to positions of power) as to what art and knowledge are. The transformative methods offered by often marginalized 21st century research-based art which challenge the grand narratives and methodologies produced and accepted by monocultural practices are reminders of the principles of permaculture ethics, which are grounded in the notion of care that, in turn, relates to practices of sharing and (re)using resources. These methods could render the art institution and university as more innovative realms of experience. Evolving from the loaded and manifold agency of culture as a form of cultivation of varied types of fields, learning from recent proposals for a radical transformation of agriculture, and using a combination of practices of listening and care with research-based arts, we might be able to interrogate Europe's postcolonial heritage in producing and validating knowledge and aesthetic epistemologies within art institutions and universities and to demand greater investigation onto how these processes impact the environment.

I would like to put forward the following hypothesis: monocultural practices in art institutions and universities adversely impact the environment. If these practices transition from mono to permacultural, via listening and caring for narratives which have been systemically ignored, then the amount and diversity of knowledge and aesthetic epistemologies will increase and contribute to local solutions for the environmental crisis that is endangering (human and natural) survival.

While the world changes rapidly, particularly in times of crises, art institutions and universities are also acknowledging the urgency for a transitioning. However, institutions seem to be failing to transform from within, in their hiring practices, "student recruitment, curriculum, recognition of art practices that acknowledge and accommodate different aesthetic epistemologies" (Mistry and Bamaso, 2020). Consequently, the framing of artistic works by institutional practices and viewpoints reveals this monocultural stance that represents colonial legacies of racial, gender, and social privilege sedimented in institutional structures that, in turn, marginalize the production and understanding of multi-aesthetic epistemologies and knowledge. While dismissing diverse visual cultures and knowledge, art institutions and universities are ignoring methods and knowledge(s) – such as alternative uses of material resources, sharing and collective practices, and oral traditions – which could be crucial in acting upon the environmental crisis. Permaculture focuses precisely on the margins: sharing techniques and ideas with and / or borrowed from agroecology, biodynamical agriculture, indigenous modes of land care, and more, permaculture offers a window into related spheres of alternative / marginal knowledge and ecological doings moving in between human and non-human realms. Furthermore, while focusing on the margins, it is rooted in an ethos of care (earth care, people care, fair share). Permaculture is then a timely intervention in support of the awareness that we live in an interconnected world, and where marginalized narratives coexist with grand narratives and which must be given equal importance. We need to unpack the manifold links in between systems, methods, and narratives that are present in the complexity of our diverse natural and human world.

Since 2020, under the impact of the global Covid-19 pandemic, the notion of care has been both practiced and theorized. While in the arts we have experienced a discursive explosion of care, we have barely put collective care into our institutional practices. Here, I will adopt ideas of design principles of permaculture in its ethos of care for / of / with marginalized narratives in an attempt to propose how art institutions and universities could shift from monocultural entities (re)presenting grand-mono-narratives towards permacultural organisms imagi(ni)ng new narratives.

Following the permaculture principle "observe and interact," through observation we are able to understand the patterns and relationships between various elements of a situation. Our modern education has trained us to specialize and dissect things into manageable pieces but in so doing we can miss the connections which lead to incorrect or less effective solutions. This is how current European priorities are set. In 2019, the European Commission set the "European Green Deal" as one of its top priorities until 2024, which means that the guidelines for the funding calls for creative industries are designed around the same priority. Within the same timeframe (2019 – 24) the Creative Europe program has aligned its support to the cultural and creative sectors with the EU anti-discrimination policy, from equal opportunities between women and men to combating racism. But the Green New Deal and the EU anti-discrimination policy alone are not enough because both fail in acknowledging their intersections, their links with European colonial legacies, and the specificities of each local context. Furthermore, while culture industries have been focusing on the environmental impact of their material activities, they have been ignoring what marginalizing diverse knowledge does to what we know about other humans and nature. The term "intersectionality" is defined as the "view that women experience oppression in varying configurations and in varying degrees of intensity. Cultural patterns of oppression are not only interrelated but are bound together and influenced by the intersectional systems of society. Examples of this include race, gender, class, ability, and ethnicity" (Crenshaw, 1989).

So far, intersectional discourse dismisses, on the one hand, how oppressed communities are often at the forefront of advocacy and action for a more sustainable and fairer planet and, on the other hand, that the decision-making powers that determine how we deal with the environment exist along gendered, class-based, ableist, and racialized lines, which means that climate justice can only happen with social and economic justice. Furthermore, intersectionality is fully anthropocentric in the sense that it doesn't consider that current challenges and regimes of oppression are affected by and affect not only humans but also the more-than-human. Just like transdisciplinarity creates new disciplinary conceptualizations, transectionality will allow the production of new knowledge from the tensions between various human and more-than-human identities and how these identities (co)inhabit within diverse local contexts of art institutions. Transectionality will enable us to see how various forms of discrimination, exploitation, and extraction in the natural and human parts of the world cannot be seen as separate from each other but need to be understood in relation to each other in the local practices of art institutions.

To move beyond the environmental impact of (artistic and cultural) material activities towards the environmental impact of marginalizing diverse knowledge via assessing the various forms of lack of diversity in art institutions and universities, we need to ask questions such as: Who gets to occupy important positions within institutions? Which power pyramids are structural and systemic? Who gets to speak / show about what which determines the processes of validation of knowledge and aesthetic epistemologies? To understand how this lack of diversity affects knowledge production and how it impacts in the environment, we need to observe and to listen to narratives that have been systemically and systematically ignored and ask: What are ways of connecting to nature and to other humans aside from dominant Western ways? What are the methodologies and knowledges that have been ignored / erased / marginalized during the colonial past?

If we can recognize that a greater knowledge lies within a diverse group of people, we can work with others to bring about the best outcomes for all involved, while acknowledging the differences (as well as needs and conditions) of each context including human and non-human. Drawing these transections between racial and gender diversity with the processes of knowledge production and how it impacts on the environment will enable us to foster, in an unprecedented way, the understanding of the links between gender, race, and the environment and, consequently, existing creative industries' policies of racial and gender diversity and representativeness in relationship to the European Green Deal. While complete change within institutions is always difficult, the presence of locally evolved models is more likely to be successful in transitioning institutional practices than a pre-designed model from the outside. Following the notions of observe and interact expressed in permaculture, a diversity of local models could naturally generate innovative elements which can cross-fertilize similar innovations across institutions, within and beyond the arts.

PRINCIPLE II:

OBTAIN A YIELD: CARING CULTURES

A yield, profit, or product(ion) function as a reward that encourages, maintains and/or replicates the system that generated the yield. In this way, successful systems spread. Permaculture practices have extended through practice-sharing, teaching, community building, and eco-social activism. Its proponents envision the ethical and political effectiveness of permaculture in the possibility of transforming people's ways of caring about everyday relations to the earth, its inhabitants, and resources (Puig de la Bellacasa, 2017). Ideas of mutual support and care for the other have existed across different times, cultures, and disciplinary fields. As the Care Collective asserts, "in order to really thrive we need caring communities. (…) in which we can support each other and generate networks of belonging. We need conditions that enable us to act collaboratively to create communities that both support our abilities and nurture our interdependencies" (2020:38). Models of care are highlighted in marginalized 21st century art by the children and grandchildren of (de)colonized communities, via methods such as storytelling, listening, and ritual.

To cite an example, in *Pia Mú / Look at me* (2018 – 22), René Tavares (1983, São Tomé, based in Lisbon) worked with the angular fishing community of São Tomé Príncipe, one of the few African communities that resisted colonialism, to reflect upon methods of resistance, how these shape(d) solidary communities and how they relate to natural and built spaces. Caring relationships between individuals, the collective, and nature also come across in *Ókakò r'Évu* (plant womb in Urhobo) (2022), by Stacey Ejiroghene Okparavero (1989, Nigeria, based in Berlin). A plant womb that transformed gradually, as seeds germinated and the womb became an evolving space where non-related people gathered to feel the life of the earth mother pulse while embodying conviviality. Exploring philosophical concepts of the embodied mind, as understood in many non-Western philosophies; thus, practicing the fact that human cognition is not only shaped by the brain, but encompassed in the body that performs cognitive tasks like conceptualization, reasoning and judgement, but also through interactions with the environment or the world at large (Ndikung, 2021), these artistic practices prompt a repositioning of relations towards coexistence and care for the (human and non-human) other.

Care is – in theory – also fundamental to curatorial practices: the Latin root of the word "curator," the verb "curare," also means "to care" and "to cure" as in "to heal." The root "cura" also refers to "sorrow," "anxiety" and "love." In the English-speaking world, historically, curators cared for a collection specific to a museum or gallery, or a historic property or heritage site. While this is a definition that many curators continue to identify with today, in the last decade the possibilities of curatorial practices have been expanded via a caring ethos: curators working against the repression and marginalization of others, and concurrently for modes of thinking about and experiencing art that are sensitive to difference on multiple levels, prompting a repositioning or transformation of relations towards coexistence and the care for the other. Nevertheless, few exhibitions in Western Europe rarely upset / cared for the broader system that pigeonholes people affected by colonialism into monocultural and essentialized categories. Large-scale art institutions and universities, which follow European governmental policies, are, in many cases, still places where the interests of economic growth predominate, deepening inequality among people of different races, genders, physical and cognitive capacities, economic and social strata. Their first and ultimate responsibility should be for social and environmental sustainability, which is to say, to care for humans and the places we inhabit. A caring institution recognizes our mutual interdependencies, that we live in community with humans and non-humans, and that, like people, institutions are living organisms without the fictional borders created in and by colonial legacies. While this acknowledging of interdependencies might be common in non-Western cultures, in which the conception of kinship often derives from the centrality of cultivating just relations with human and non-human relatives and with the earth, most Western cultures, following their colonial histories, are hierarchical and grounded in extraction and exploitation of the (human and non-human) other. Creating communities that can and want to care means amplifying spaces that are public, that are held and created in common, that are shared and collaborative, that grow without walls, rather than those designed for the sake of private capital. To do this is to create a sharing infrastructure, which involves mutual support and sharing community material and immaterial resources. Drawing on a range of caring arrangements common in other periods or places, and based on alternative kinship structures, we could put forward new practices of radical care to experiment with methods and understandings of care. A transformation towards caring systems requires recognition of different artistic and scientific practices and diverse sources of evidence, including new ways of seeing, sharing, of knowledge production and exchange based on transdisciplinary, cross-scalar, and participatory approaches. These approaches need to draw from non-Western science, Western, and Indigenous, traditional, and experiential knowledge systems to foster the co-creation of evidence, generate new qualitative and quantitative insights and narratives, and support the development of enabling policies. The results of this science, aesthetic epistemologies, and knowledge exchange need to be shared – not just in peer-reviewed articles and in exhibition catalogues but between different institutional system actors and through listening to stories and looking at visual narratives.

USE AND VALUE DIVERSITY, EDGES, AND THE MARGINAL: IMAGI(NI)NG ALTERNATIVE NARRATIVES AND FUTURES

Diversity within species and populations is critical to the long-term stability of systems. In light of critical global challenges, such as climate change and food and nutrition security, there is an urgent need to maintain and enhance agricultural biodiversity. This also extends to human communities: for permaculture, the conservation of at least some of the great diversity of languages and cultures on the planet is arguably as important as the conservation of biodiversity. The need for diversity of knowledge production is very clear in agriculture: inherent to resilient seed systems is the ongoing, historic, and dynamic process of domestic crop cultivation and innovation in response to changing ecological, social, and economic conditions. This immense service is only possible because of the rich systems of knowledge, culture, and ecology stewardship held by Indigenous Peoples and smallholder farming communities who have managed, protected, and defended seed diversity across our planet. Their evolutionary services provide humanity with a wealth of seed diversity adapted to local contexts and spread across diverse global ecosystems, increasing resiliency to shocks and changes such as climate disruption. Farmer-managed and community-based seed systems need to be valued for their important contributions to agricultural biodiversity, food security, and nutrition.

Diverse and inclusive environments where a diversity of perspectives is valued not only relates to knowledge sharing and production, they also go beyond the context of agricultural diversity: diverse environments breed academic excellence as well as artistic and cultural production (Mistry and Mabaso, 2021) because they enable the production of diverse knowledge(s) and aesthetic epistemologies, which, in turn, are needed to respond to the environmental crisis that is putting at risk not only human and natural diversity but, above all, survival. Universities are implanted in the interstices between theory and practice; between the world as we know it and as we think it can become (Braceli, 2022) just as art that, in its speculative practices, greets us with alternative possible futures (Santos, 2021), in between facts and fiction, as a means of critique and provocation of such futures (cf. Helgason and Smyth, 2020). Art institutions and universities hold the potential to embody Boaventura de Sousa Santos' postulation that "Another Knowledge is Possible" and vying to his arguments that there is no social justice without global cognitive justice. As de Sousa Santos states, the exclusions, oppressions, and discriminations produced by global capitalism have not only had economic, social, and political effects upon the world, but have also had detrimental cultural and epistemological effects (de Sousa Santos, 2008 as cited in Ndikung, 2021).

While art institutions and universities hold the potential to create alternative narratives – via aesthetic epistemologies and knowledge production – for what the future of the world can be, it is also important to note that, current (grand) narratives emerging in European art institutions and universities are grounded in visual cultures' systems and models of selection and merit (both for the public activities, such as exhibitions and course syllabi, and for the not so visible parts, namely the recruiting practices, not to mention the fees for higher education) solely based on Western patriarchal criteria, which still echo European colonial legacies. This implies that a large spectrum of voices, aesthetics, and knowledge remain muted and made invisible. Following the understanding of marginal and edges of permacultures, the marginal and invisible aspects of any system should not only be recognized and conserved, but expanded to increase productivity and stability. The inclusion of marginalized visual and oral narratives is key to understand the multidimensions of the world as it is but also to think how it can be.

When thinking about art and education as spaces for exchange and broadening perspectives, we must consider the complexity of the issue between opacity and visibility, since both are strategically articulated in the history of humankind to contribute to the world as we (think we) know it, where there is a scenario organized to make things visible and invisible, audible and silent. Twenty-first century art of the children of empire offers an entrance into marginalized narratives that are systemically and systematically not listened to and that rarely make it to the books from which Europeans learn and produce art, curatorial, and educational projects that, in turn, shape European art institutions and universities. Taking up the history and territory of former colonies, much of the work of the children of empire combine ethnography and speculation to unpack the frictions and fictions imprinted upon both natural and built environments and their inhabitants. Revealing the relationships between colonialism, postcolonialism, and the manifold of -isms of modern and contemporary art history, transformative methods offered by marginalized 21st century visual art denounce the human consumption and destruction of the natural environment and indigenous communities, while highlighting narratives that have been ignored, or erased, from what we have come to understand and validate as history. In so doing, these artists have chosen to explore other media that embody, produce, and disseminate other types of knowledges. Their practices translate the fact that knowledge production is not a linear process and it encompasses all parts of our bodies as well as of our surroundings, which, in turn, are inhabited by other human and non-human entities. Visually analyzing their work, listening carefully to their narratives that have been systemically and systemically put aside, will allow us not to create another/ parallel canon, but – as Bonaventure Soh Bejeng Ndikung beautifully puts it – to decanonize the notion of the canon as a whole (2021).

BIBLIOGRAPHY

Bell, Richard (2022). "Bell's Theorem (Reductio ad Infinitum): Contemporary Art – It's a White Thing!". *E-flux*, issue 129, September 2022. https://www.e-flux.com/journal/129/486788/bell-s-theorem-reductio-ad-infinitum-contemporary-art-it-s-a-white-thing/

Braceli, Miguel (2022). "The naked school". *La Scuela*. https://laescuela.art/en/campus/library/essays/the-naked-school-miguel-braceli Accessed August 2nd 2022.

Care Collective (2020). *Care Manifesto*. London and New York: Verso.

Crenshaw, Kimberle (1989) "Demarginalizing the Intersection of Race and Sex: A Black Feminist Critique of Antidiscrimination Doctrine, Feminist Theory and Antiracist Politics," *University of Chicago Legal Forum*: Iss. 1, Article 8.
Available at: http://chicagounbound.uchicago.edu/uclf/vol1989/iss1/8

de Sousa Santos, Boaventura et al.: (2008). "Opening Up the Canon of Knowledge and Recognition of Difference," in Boaventura de Sousa Santos (ed) *Another Knowledge Is Possible: Beyond Northern Epistemologies*, London: Verso.

Helgason, Ingi and Smyth, Michael (2020). "Ethnographic Fictions: Research for Speculative Design". Conference on Designing Interactive Systems (Companion Volume), pp. 203 – 207.

Mistry and Bamaso (2021). "Introductory Comments: initiatives and strategies." *On Curating*. Issue 49, 2 – 10.

Ndikung, Bonaventure Soh Bejeng (2021). SAVVY Contemporary The Laboratory of Form-Ideas: A CONCEPT reloaded. Berlin: SAVVY Contemporary.

Persic, Ana, and Martin, Gary (2008). Links between biological and cultural diversity: report of the International Workshop. Paris: UNESCO.

Puig de la Bellacasa, María (2017). *Matters of Care: speculative ethics in more than human worlds*. Minneapolis: University of Minnesota Press. ISBN 978-1-5179-0064-9 (hc) | ISBN 978-1-5179-0065-6 (pb)

Shannan M. Grant RD and MSc(c) and BSc (2007). "The Importance of Biodiversity in Crop Sustainability: A Look at Monoculture", *Journal of Hunger & Environmental Nutrition*, 1:2, 101 – 109, DOI: 10.1300/J477v01n02_07

Santos, Luísa (2022a). "Telling a story of silence(s) in three parts". In Santos, Luísa (ed.). (2022). *Cultures of Silence*. London: Routledge.

Santos, Luísa and Maurício, Ana Fabíola (2020). "Offsetting Sameness: Notes Towards Artistic and Institutional Polysemy and Practices of/on Monocultures and Multicultures". *Considering monoculture*. Brussels: DeBuren, 28th February 2020.

Santos, Luísa e Maurício, Ana Fabíola (2021). Talk tower for Forough Forrokzhad. Lisboa e Estocolmo: CECC e Tensta Konsthall. ISBN: 978-989-54428-4-3

Santos, Luísa (2022b). "Calls for listening: a tribute to untold micro-narratives". In LaBelle, Brandon (ed.) (2022). *The Listening Biennial Reader*, vol. 1. Berlin: Errant Bodies Press.

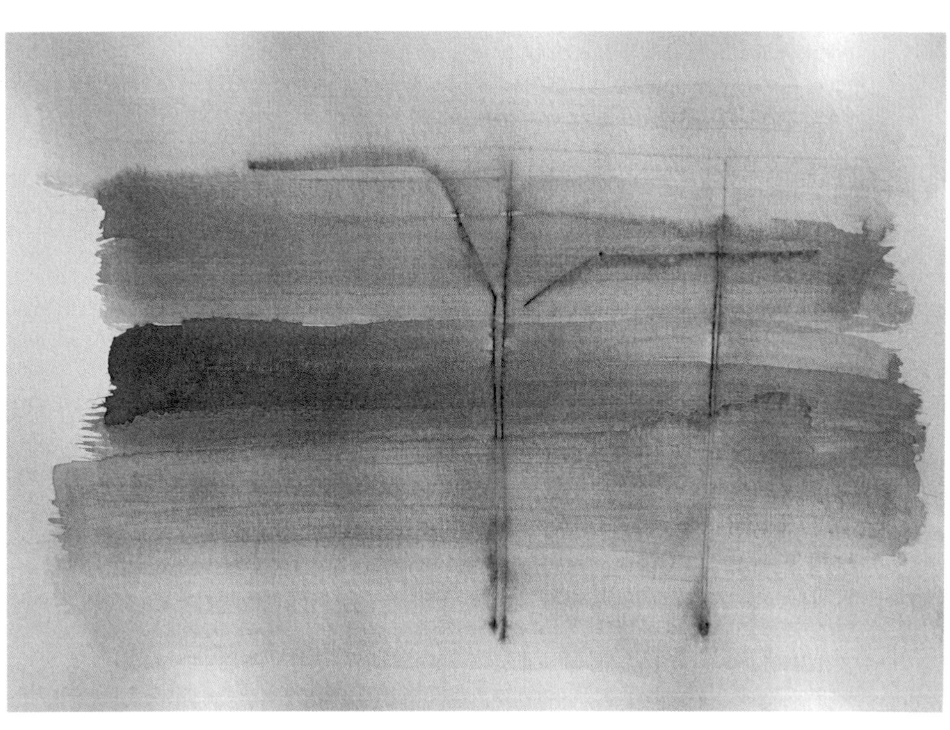

BRANDON LABELLE

Drumming Water – on Wet Sound

"There … beside the palm tree …"
"I see it! How far does it extend?"
"Into the alley, you know, behind the liquor store"
"I never noticed … – near where the surf breaks?"
dropping coins into the well
Waiting, waiting … for the echo
hands shoved into rough pockets;
lights aglow from the faraway city casting
across the dark churning expanse

THE CLIFFS

I remember how important empty fields, abandoned sites, the cliffs and the beach, as well as pathways that crossed in and out of the light – how these were vital to being a teenager. Growing up in southern California I was fortunate to be part of a group of friends whose desires and imaginations echoed my own. In short, we were generally aligned with what others termed the dropouts, the trouble makers, the dreamers – teenagers captured by existential literature, punk music, the golden sun, and landscapes of the night. In this situation we found ourselves at odds with dominant patterns of the social milieu, leading to search for alternative territories. By way of the particular emptiness stemming from experiences of not fitting-in, we mapped hidden geographies in between the articulation of streets, locating interstitial areas conducive to hanging out, as well as trajectories of escape in and around home and school. We hid things in bushes, we kept clothes in trees; we knew where the cops were and where the parents would be; and we kept to the darkness, often spending nights listening to the ocean and each other.

> *The darkness in which things may find refuge*
> *The darkness in which to imagine other worlds*
> *The darkness in which life and love find new possibilities*
> *undercover and out of sight*
> *The darkness of shared listening*

In particular, we found refuge in empty fields, abandoned sites, and especially along the cliffs and beaches. I clearly remember instances when, on particularly difficult days, we would congregate along the cliffs to follow the disappearing sun and its orange light, or after a night of partying at a house of a friend whose parents no doubt were out of town, we'd seek the natural rhythms of the ocean, feeling the sand under us as we fell asleep, with the wet fog billowing in from the dark horizon. These are memories that still resound, and that I sense as a foundation, a fundament, a bass-note, to a certain structure of feeling I carry with me, and which carries a deeply held orientation toward sound and listening as providing refuge. Even today, I can say that my own practice and thinking, which have been formed around an *acoustic leaning*, are grounded in the potentiality of sonic escape, one that enables the crafting of other worlds, the configuring of unlikely affiliations, that is, a form of refuge and resistance to mechanisms of social ordering. Rather, this acoustic leaning is a leaning toward, what I may roughly define as, an *anarchic* approach.

Following these memories, I want to consider how, within this acoustic leaning, those formative experiences are not only marked by a sonic relation or matter, but moreover carry the presence of water, especially that of the ocean. There, around the angst and loneliness of teenage life, as part of the friendships that gave support, and that gave me the chance to keep going, the ocean was ever-present. Having grown up in an area whose topography is defined by rolling hills that feed down toward the ocean, ending in jagged cliffs that wrap themselves around a peninsula, the ocean served as a beacon and steady point of orientation: no matter where in the hills we were, whether in certain ravines or across open fields, or along winding streets, we could always sense where the ocean was. From the sound of its waves to the wind carrying its salt, the winter fogs that would roll over the hills and drown us in a grey ambiguity, or the barking of seals which at night sounded eerily from below the cliffs – and how the setting sun directed us, pulling us toward the cliffs to meditate upon the closing day: no matter, the ocean could always be relied on.

Seeking the company of the ocean was to find respite from the turmoil of a social existence; it was to be reborn by way of an aqueous intensity, one whose ceaseless movements would wash over the angular architectures of an emerging masculinity, contouring its rigidity into something more tender, fluid and sympathetic. Seeking solace in the ocean's elemental presence was to return to one's body – to recover its fullness from the alienating effects of socialization; it was to find again the body as an ecology of sensation, a story of the heart, opening onto ways of reconnecting with primary rhythms and reasons. *These were sensations set in motion by the flows and force of an Oceanic Being.*

While I am oriented by way of sound, I'm also oriented by way of the ocean: these two together, which becomes suggestive for a theory of *wet sound.*

The streets thread themselves across dry hills The days like brittle grass holding against passing seasons with their storms and broken edges – under the skin molecular vibrating the nerves cells alive to voices the laughter showered in blue The deep tussle of the body finding its way pressed grating against vocabularies economies identities and These other things glimpsed in the waves violent and restorative and elemental The story to be made and made again whispered into the dreaming life through misty afternoons nights reverberant with a watery ongoingness *O take me take me into your deep world dripping dripping* The hours dripping nestling amidst dry hills Brittle grass against the wet ear as they roll back The body that unfolds for itself for others guided by the flow

WET SOUND

The notion of wet sound makes reference to the field of acoustics and how levels of reverberation are designated by way of wetness as well as dryness. Wet sound captures the intensity of reverberation and can be followed as a suggestive link between the potential expansiveness of sound and wateriness. Such a link opens onto material resonances, in terms of sonic spatialization, as well as psychological poetics – is not sound that which carries us elsewhere, inciting the imagination? I may elaborate this relation by appreciating the ways in which reverberant acoustical experiences produce feelings of immersion: reverberation occurs as a wash of sound, already suggestive for appreciating the connection between sound and water. The immersiveness of wet sound signals a state of indecipherability or lack of clarity, where singularities merge, lose definition. Reverberation pulls things together, or diffuses their borders, making of them a *flood* of information, thereby moving the signal toward noise. While reverberation is essential to listening experiences, in terms of bringing life to sound as a situated or placial event, it can easily tip toward annoyance, breakdown. Fundamentally, wet sound places one on an acoustic spectrum that moves from proximity, closeness, where dryness creates intimacy, to distance, immersion, where wetness induces feelings of transcendence – this is easily found by following the acoustics of cathedrals, where reverberation puts one in touch with the heavens (and the logic of spiritual connection). The reverberant qualities of such architectures lift listeners above the material realities of mundane society, to guide toward the metaphysical sacredness of the divine. By way of such perspectives, wet sound may be heard to carry or evoke a *reverberant potentiality*: this is a conduit or portal by which to grasp a world beyond the immediate; by way of the wash of sound, one is transported, carried, put in touch with an elsewhere. As such, it may figure a sense of spatial possibility, in terms of the crafting of escape routes and the finding of unlikely affiliations, and it may engender a poetic horizon, one that affords spiritual rescue: to be lifted by a noise greater than oneself. Wet sound is never singular, rather, it binds singularities into a greater flow or mix, diffusing boundaries and lending to new unexpected assemblages. It also fosters leaks and spills, suggesting ways of making new configurations; it is by way of the reverberant potentiality of wet sound that emergent community formations may be fostered, felt, crafted and elaborated.

These are perspectives and ideas that return me to experiences of teenage life, and how it is that the cliffs, the beach, provided refuge to a small group of friends. I'm tending to appreciate how such refuge was conditioned by an ongoing relation to the ocean, the movements of tides, the rhythmic companionship offered by nuanced patterns of currents and waves, not to mention the storms, the crashing and ebbing, mists and fogs, all of which give expression to the dynamic qualities of wet sound. These oceanic sonorities and matters that would wash over us, that would guide in times of crisis, that would assuage in moments of ache, to afford material paths or flows by which other orientations could emerge. Noises that made it possible to disappear, to lose oneself in their reverberant potentiality as a means of finding a body for oneself, especially attuned to a *tidalectical* imaginary (following Kamau Brathwaite). By way of wet sound and its related movements, a feeling for being a *citizen of the world* emerged – to be located and dislocated at the same time. To participate in a fluid construct through which all bodies touch, are made.

"It doesn't matter, it doesn't matter …"
"I know, I know …"
Candy moon on this vacant night, candy touch he dreams skin bare to the nipping wind as they go down, under, even though even though win-

ter feels like a frigid envelope tightly held diving nonetheless swimming swimming lunging thrashing against seaweed beds rough stones the relentless dark it is darker still with salt pouring into clasped eyes and lips he could go further feeling into the waves it all fruity rich with strange blossoms slippery tentacles ancient truths Brian singing into cavernous waves like a crazed pirate picking lyrics from unknown depths and hallucinatory mind That stings holds calming the nerves *I wish I was a headlight on a northbound train* ... nothing but dark splashed fractals of moonlight Keith bare chested on the rocks stringing sea creatures for supper right from the riptide his feet scratched and chapped the rough barnacles long hair strings caught in starlight like guiding rays the skin that would collect warmth through the summer sending currents of electricity all around "O dear, tell us of the crashing stars, the bursting universe?" "I see you ... I see you" Rusted metals from lost ships tearing against time holding the sand under fingernails bitten through the days

THIRST

I want to take a step back, or further in, to move from the oceanic expanse, and the rapturous fullness of wet sound, toward the materiality of water itself: to find within its liquidity the basis for self-determination. While the reverberant potentiality offered by the deep force of the ocean gave support to the daily strains of youth, to make a link between noise and freedom, sonic escape and cosmo-elemental identity, there are other facets to the story, especially in terms of *finding the voice*. For even as the sounding ocean provided an escape route, a means of transport and transformation, one inevitably had to muster the courage to go on – to find ways of being a social subject, to leave behind the cliffs, the beach, to step back into the daily structures of language and meaning, institutions and history, not to mention the loneliness, the fights. The acoustic affordances harnessed by way of reverberation can be found equally in how it gives traction to speech and voicing: reverberation functions as a support, a type of auditory scaffolding by which vocalization finds its footing – in lifting up, wet sound also carries the voice: it may aid in times when raising the volume is urgently needed. Yet, I'm also led to think in what ways one searches for water so as to support the voice, to work against the dryness of the tongue, to overcome a parched throat – a cracked voice is one that falters as it tries to pass across the larynx, one that sticks in the throat, perhaps when confronted by a dominating authority, or when language seems to fall short. Water lubricates, assuages, replenishes, it prepares the voice: one pauses, to pick up a glass of water, setting the conditions for the voice to come.

Within scenes and situations of estrangement, one grows thirsty – it might be said that we gravitated to the ocean because we were in need of water: in need of its sonorities, its liquid balm, its immersive intervention as well as restorative influence; to overcome a parched throat, a dry season, finding within its reverberant potentiality the means to speak. A sound by which to guide our own.

Yet, wet sound is not only that which supplies the voice with lubrication or assistance; it can be found to function as the medium for speech itself – to speak *through* water. Such critical concerns find a point of reference in the Afrofuturistic work of Drexciya, an electronic music duo from Detroit (James Stinson (1969 – 2002) and Gerald Donald). Active throughout the 1990s, Drexciya's music is built upon a self-styled myth that tells of an underwater country, Drexciya, populated by children born from pregnant African women who were thrown off of slave ships while crossing the Atlantic. These are African children who adapted to breathing underwater, forming their own self-proclaimed nation. A type of Black Atlantis, the story of Drexciya gestures toward Paul Gilroy's theories of the Black Atlantic as a middle passage whose violences come to produce complex imaginaries – a double consciousness that unsettles or troubles fixed identities and ethnic narratives of origin (found also in Eduard Glissant's notion of *echos monde*, as a poetics of relation emerging from the oceanic complexities of passage and colonial constructs). By way of the Black Atlantic we may hear another type of oceanic reverberation, one that engenders musical hybridities and noisy junctions constituted by the rhythms and tonalities carried

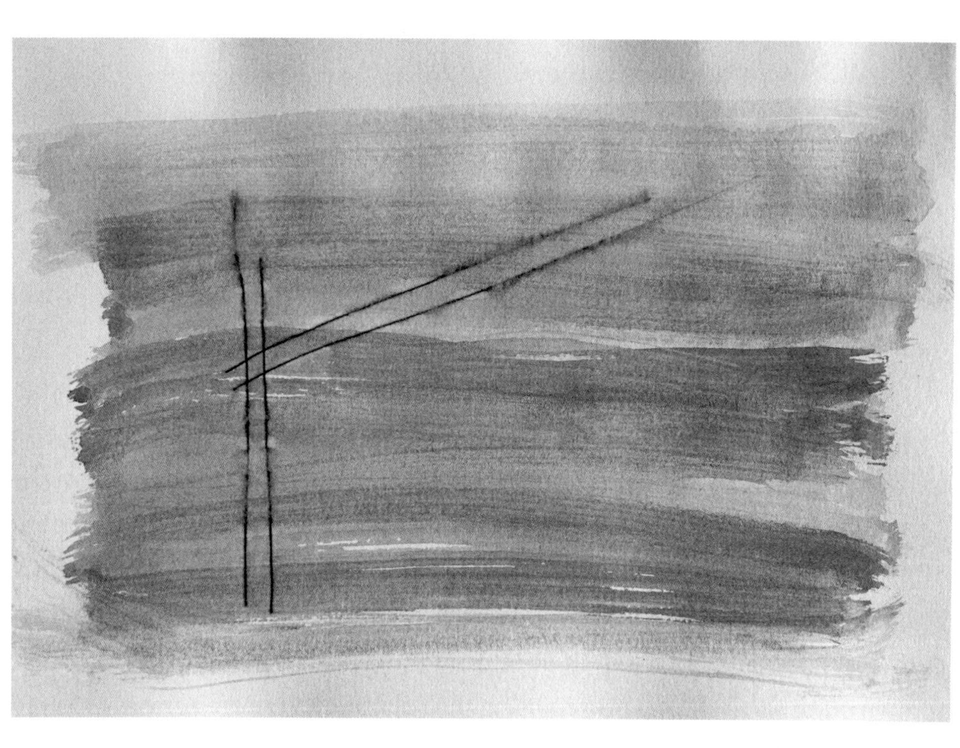

across the water, to take up residence in the localities, economies and musical cultures of modernity. From the coasts of Caribbean islands to the New World metropolises and plantations, from West African villages to European ports, the Black Atlantic as Gilroy highlights is resonant with sonic passages and rhythmic intersections. This can be heard, as but one example, in the music of Reggae, which originally combines instruments of European culture with drums from Africa, filling the dance halls of Jamaica with their syncopated rhythms and chants – lyrics voiced in the *patois* of island creole and that herald the coming of a Black Messiah. These are the echoes constituting Glissant's poetics of relation, giving shape to a reverberant construct awash with oceanic force.

In what way do these passages and musics lend to theories of wet sound and related forms of refuge found by way of the ocean? While the ocean may offer solace, or give way to cultures of dynamic sound, it may equally drown some in its unapologetic expanse. Finding emancipatory conduits in wet sound is tensed by the colonial enterprises that would demarcate the Atlantic into myriad trading routes, cutting into its immersive wholeness, and the wholeness of African bodies and communities, with the brutality of imperial greed.

Such oceanic violences find an additional point of reference, this time in the country of Chile whose coastal waters became a graveyard of the Disappeared: persons kidnapped and tortured under the Pinochet dictatorship and thrown from helicopters into the ocean. Often strapped to metal rails so as to pull the bodies to the ocean floor, these Disappeared have come to haunt the nation, drawing out a complex culture of memorialization for the missing. This finds expression in a film by the artist Enrique Ramírez. Titled *Brises* (*Breezes*, 2008), the film follows the sudden appearance of a man who walks the streets of the capital drenched in water; with his shirt and coat dripping, and his steps leaving a watery trail across the asphalt, the man takes a determined path to the presidential palace all the while a voice-over meditates on loss, rupture and broken history, telling of childhood memories, the sadness the sea carries, and the disappearances numbing the nation. Ramírez's symbolic figure is that of the Disappeared risen from the ocean, brought back to enter again the city of Santiago – a watery figure that returns to the palace to reclaim a place at the heart of the nation. Importantly, *Brises* follows water as what both haunts as well as heals, claiming lives while slowly, over time, enabling a process of cleansing. While the music of Drexciya can be heard as the amplification of an Afrofuturistic world underwater, Ramírez stages a poetic intervention onto the streets, delivering the submerged citizen back to the capital. Both draw forth an oceanic song of redemption, capturing the resistant current of a tidalectical imaginary.

> "If you look up, it's like all the plasma of the universe is moving … you think it's empty, like some type of nothingness, but it's so full, it's a mass of stuff but we just can't see it, we're always looking for the thing you know, vision can't detect something so vast or it can't see into it because it's too deep, that's the mystery he talked about and that defied the thinking at the time … but I still wonder about what is out there you know, the life of things …" His voice grows tired pressed by the persistent winds the sand whistling he lies back falls into the dreamy earth "… who knows where all this sand comes from …" as he dozes off smiling brown hair caught in the corner of his mouth

Can we think further as to water's particular sonority? As what offers an elemental synchronization, an immersion in the primary bath of wet sound? And which acts as a balm when confronted by the world's harsh realities? Engendering a new movement vocabulary, to "swim beyond the situatedness of our own bodies" (Neimanis 4). Moreover, water emerges as a passage itself, a medium by which to craft an alternative voice, an alternative nation or city: to recover precisely what may go missing or is forced under. To breathe or speak by way of water is to be submerged in a politics of capture and renewal, figured as a negotiation with the socio-economic operations of The Ship (and what it might mean to be "contained" as well as thrown over) and where the oceanic expanse of a potential freedom keeps one going. Such watery tensions are expressive of a planetary force – which is never purely nourishing, never simply restorative: finding solace in the potentiality of wet sound is to plunge into the thrashing, overpowering matters of Oceanic Being. To swim in such immersive power is to know of the body as vulnerable, a natural vitality in sync with a living and dying world. It might be to sound a livable life not by way of the acoustics of spatial volume, but through the mysterious, enduring and awesome medium of water itself which also keeps one close to the blood coursing through the body.

These are coordinates to wet sound and its reverberant potentiality, and which open onto a hydro-acoustic episteme – ways of orienting and knowing that pull from the land, the cliffs, the beach, drawing into its tides and mists all sorts of matters, languages, musics, to configure a tidalectical poetics of fluid listening, of deep time and memory, loss, resistance and renewal, the continual ebb and flow. This might be what we felt as we gathered along the cliffs in southern California, attuning by way of the ocean to one's own watery existence, sensing the pools of a turbulent imaginary, something that flows back across planetary time and that rushes forward as well, to lap against the horizon mixing all types of matter and meaning – keeping the motion, the wave of being going. Water reminds by way of its ever-shifting movements the degree to which bodies are *stirred* rather than fixed, giving way to a swirling co-constitution of things and each other.

While the sonorities of Oceanic Being touched and trembled, resonated and nourished us, it may have been the slow unfolding of fog that would pour in from the ocean to fall over the cliffs and hills which gave us a particular means for taking cover. It might be said that the fog would come to carry the ocean onto the land, bringing its salty waves over the houses, the streets, the shopping malls and civic buildings, to obscure and diffuse the lines of a particular social geometry: by way of the fog it became possible to glimpse another type of architecture, to shift from the hard edges of social meaning to the vague contours of an ambient commons – to grasp the reverberant potentiality of wet sound, following it into the fog that would hang over the hills as a *grey air*, dropping its misty beads across the skin, the eyes, moistening the hair and ground. This was a form of atmospheric exit found in diffusion, a *becoming-fog* ... and ... which manifested ... in acts of poetic world-making ... the creative reworking of a social configuration ... There along the cliffs, washed over by the sounding ongoingness of the ocean held by the night, and drenched in the grey fog wetting the skin, the voice, a small group of friends were to find the courage to go on by way of shared vulnerability ... a sharing always tensed and tenuous ... *stumbling this way and that way in shopping malls and cinemas and liquor stores with video games stealing cans of beer the stupid laughter late at night hanging out behind the video store eating pizza slices sitting bored in classrooms trying to catch something a line a vision a wave ...*

While the reverberant potentiality of wet sound gave way to a sense of being a citizen of the world, a planetary subject, a hydro-commoner, the ambience of fog, with its grey misty dimensions, instilled an affective tonality whose sympathies engendered deep feelings of interdependency however unspoken. Awash in the tidal movements and watery sonorities, and drenched in the soft touch of fog, friendship and love and hanging out and on together became principles and practices, figuring a *tender-logic* by which to find again and again the body as a natural power of connection. To be a citizen of the world was to live as a swimmer.

ISLANDS

From within the mists of oceanic matter, dimensions are to be found. Grey zones. Zones of refuge. Places or dwellings configured by way of the tonalities and diffuse borders of oceanic matter. That emerge under the stars, in nights awash with deep fogs within which human society slows, is held captive, halted. And which supports ways of getting lost. Here new visions strangely appear; unexpected, unlikely perspectives whose blurry and ever-shifting angles trace an altogether different type of structure. A misty-sphere lending to new paths of orientation, new languages and partnerships – from out of the fog and reverberant flood of wet sound one discovers an array of others. These are the lost souls, the drifting communities, the disappearing anarchists and swimmers who drop off, seeking other trajectories and economies, modes of being and surviving beyond the defined grid of social meaning increasingly captive to neoliberal economies. Against the new world order that would emerge and take hold in the 1980s, and which marks the time of teenage life, the left over hippies and leftist radicals dotting the California coast and deserts would converge with the new punks who replaced surfboards for skateboards, taking to the streets with disaffected energy. There were also the Hollywood rockers and new romantics, as well as the new tribalism trickling down from San Francisco, those who would appropriate the junk-culture of the cold war, turning the end of history into a new pyrotechnic commons. It was there in the fog, and the roaring ocean whose deep thunders would turn over and over in our minds as we slept along the cliffs, drifting off to the watery rhythms punctuating our dreams, it was there that the noise started to make sense. A new sonic order. And which began to manifest as an aesthetic. A noise music. A grey form.

These were the vague perspectives or ever-shifting coordinates giving shape to an emerging dimension, a scene, a body, putting all our angst into the configuration of something. A place of no place, a rhythm that would run away from itself, a lyric not of words but of vibration. To chart islands of refuge. An archipelago whose noisy resonances would mask its own presence, keeping itself hidden. In the fog. Others would also come, new friends, new partners – islands are always home to the dropouts, the runaways, the marooned and the lonely. Those who wash ashore to find each other against or because of the odds. Those who cannot hold on, who cannot function according to the time signatures and spatial partitions of a contemporary system. Those who take to the fog, guided by the undefined immersiveness of wet sound. The vibration and reverberation. That pulls at the body, the imagination.

Following these movements and perspectives, it is not surprising that as teenagers we gravitated to music; not only as listeners or fans, but as players. At a certain moment, this group of friends started to pick up instruments, to come together as a band. We moved from hanging out at the cliffs at night to making music, turning spaces of the home into oceans of noise, becoming-natatorial. Jamming together became another type of swimming; we replaced the guiding force of oceanic reverberation with a self-defined interruptive wash – we made our own fog, one that could disturb the structures and social meanings surrounding, unsettling the foundation that we could only intuitively identify but whose imposition we felt in our bodies. Music was an act of survival, it was a work aimed at shifting the time signatures and spatial partitions shaping the stories we may live and tell. For myself, this found guidance by way of drumming, a drumming-swimming that took to the noisy-waters as if born anew. The drums became a material means for reconfiguring things: to lose myself in the emerging pulse of a new body, a body not necessarily without organs, but rather, one with gills. Rhythm against rhythm, where the hand, the stick, the skin were thrust into a noisy dispute with dominant patterns – these were the emergent sensations that would help recover the body as water, as flow. And where the band would come to function as an oceanic family of friends, one that would wash together individual loneliness giving way to love and rebelliousness – a music that would send its disjointed, distorted flows across all this ordered terrain. This was a form of *musicking* that carried the reverberant potentiality of wet sound brought back from the cliffs, the beach, to resound through the neighborhood, the home, to hold together in distorted currents and breaks.

*

I am swimming, in the waves that endlessly return us to ourselves; that call us back, to fall again into currents of memory; stories held and carried in the waters of the body, and whose own tides oscillate mysteriously, rising suddenly in certain moments and receding at others; water may flow as a kind of archival medium, a liquid library whose myths remain like threads or seaweeds, planted in the earth of bone, the matters of mineral, tissue, susceptible to the flows and fevers of bodily being; waves shaped by passions as they splash against terrestrial forms, that move across geologies of somatic living, lapping lapping

From the oceanic sonorities of wet sound to the misty obscurity of grey air, from the sonic junctions of a shipped modernity to the ambient fogs of a diffuse identity, the hydro-acoustic may emerge as an acoustic tethered to the ongoingness of imperial work – that sounds forth from within the reverberant hulls replete with their global matters and products, with their socializing mechanisms and containments – while equally spilling over, in the leaks, the fogs, the misty voices and collective sympathies that resound from below and give onto other channels, other routes. These are acoustic behaviors that suggest a tidalectical bodily sense of being, one that follows in the currents of an oceanic form of listening, lapping, lapping. A listening that moves by way of liquid economies and solidarities, the watery matters carrying the memories, the music, splashed with the mud of imperial work as well as all those noises that give notice. That cut their own grooves and journeys.

> He used to walk endless miles across hills dusted with summer heat the smell of fennel bushes catching bright reflections from the never-ending blue ocean filling the horizon giving way to thoughts, dreams, visions finding paths into the ravines ditches full of flowers suddenly where some would climb *kissing kissing* finding out about tomorrow with salt in his pocket held over from summer days he would hold in his fingers now and again grinding the crystals into his pores stepping to rhythms that became integral like vibrating marrow *three four, three four* a type of wave-gait set to deep flows *carrying him* these were Reasons "the depths … the depths" he used to chant under his breath like a mantra or set of watery lyrics to open the way

BIBLIOGRAPHY

Brathwaite, Kamau (1973). *The Arrivants: A New World Trilogy*. Oxford: Oxford University Press.
Gilroy, Paul (1993). *The Black Atlantic: Modernity and Double Consciousness*. London: Verso Books.
Glissant, Edouard (1997). *Poetics of Relation*. Ann Arbor: University of Michigan Press.
Neimanis, Astrida (2019). *Bodies of Water: Posthuman Feminist Phenomenology*. New York: Bloomsbury Academy.

JAMES WEBB

A series of personal questions addressed to the North Sea

A series of personal questions addressed to the North Sea is a recent edition in the ongoing artwork, *A series of personal questions.* Started in 2016, this series constitutes spoken questions being posed to specific objects and spaces. The artwork takes the form of the presentation of the subject/object in question, in this case the North Sea, and an audio speaker placed in relation to them.

The audio speaker broadcasts spoken questions written specifically for, and addressed to, the North Sea. No answers are written, given, or suggested; each question lingers, unanswered for approximately 12 seconds before the next question is posed.

The North Sea has long been a source of life, a contingent link between land-masses, and a living border: a key concern in historical and contemporary sociopolitical discourse.

From extracted oil and natural gas to contested fishing rights, the "Morimaru" as the Celts named it, is a site of ecological wonder and calamity, untold and unseen ecosystems, and projected, poetic longing.

This series has been presented as installations and performances worldwide with various objects, including 5 litres of Nigerian crude oil, an original set of Rorschach plates from 1921, and a Roman coin from 70 CE. Recent editions have been exhibited at the Monheim Triennale, the 16th Biennale de Lyon, and the inaugural Biennale of Islamic Arts. This particular version of the artwork is designed to travel to different locations that border the North Sea and be presented site-specifically there.

Listed below is an excerpt of the transcription of the live presentation of the artwork at the Listening Academy in Bergen in October 2022.

*

*The following are a series of personal questions addressed to the North Sea.
I address the sea directly.*

By what title would you like to be addressed?
What sort of knowing is possible between us?
Who, or what, was here before, and will be after?
What feelings persist from 150-million years ago?
What memories remain from when your landmasses were flooded
        20,000 years ago?
What is sleeping in your depths that no one has seen before?
Where is your absence most keenly felt?
Where is your presence feared?
Which conditions feel temporary?

Where have your needs led you?

What are you telling us when your waters run into our towns?

What do our troubles look like to you?

Who do you answer to?

*Which of the songs that sought to appease you, if any, were acceptable
to you?*

*What conversations go on between you and the shores that embrace
you?*

What are you separated from?

*What do you think of these human-made borders? In reality, where are,
or – what are your limits?*

*To what should European governance entitle its governors with
regards to you and your vast ecosystems?*

*How can the European Maritime Safety Agency, tasked with coordi-
nating sea traffic through you, better understand your needs?*

What do you make of the United Kingdom leaving the European Union?

How do you feel about the sewage they are pumping into your waters?

*What should be done about the countries that are responsible for over-
fishing in your depths?*

*What are our prejudices preventing us from understanding about you?
How can we be helpful to you?*

*What recollections do you have from when – what we understand as –
your kelp forests were formed?*

How should we interpret your image in our dreams?

What did the stars look like when you were young?

What are the important events that shaped your thalassic sexuality?

What was it like when the Sand Gaper first entered your presence?

How many full moons have you seen rise?

What is the moon to you?

*What was life on Doggerland like before, what we understand to be, a
tsunami drowned the area and separated Great Britain from
the European continent 8,000 years ago?*

What became of deities like Ægir and Rán when people stopped honouring them? What did their sea-worshipping cults mean to you?

How do you think humans can recover from Romanticism?

Why is your friendship fatal to so many young poets?

Which of the major cities on your coasts might you swallow first?

What do you think will be our future fossils?

What was life like before oil was discovered deep within you?

What does it feel like when oil is sucked from below your benthic communities?

What are you going to do now that, what we might call, the Capitalist-cene, Cthulucene, Anthropocene is all around us?

In what ways have you been shaped by human leisure?

In what ways have you been fashioned by military expansion?

In what ways have you been organised by human obsessions of scarcity?

What identities, personalities, and interpretations have been forced upon you?

Whose history is missing in this conversation?

What questions should we be asking those who have written your story?

If they are not a myth, and even if they are, what might the Selki and magical folk want in order to live to their fullest desires?

What is the myth from the Leviathan's point of view?

Whose passage to their loved ones did you create?

Whose yearning for oblivion did you facilitate?

How many political 'end games' have you witnessed?

How far have we come since King Cnut?

What did you do with the body of King Magnus IV?

How should we interpret your flooding of, what is now called, Verdronken Land van Reimerswaal on the 5th of November 1530?

What information did you extract from the wreck of the Russian frigate named Alexander Nevsky?

How many ships are sailing on you right now?

How many undisclosed drones and fighter jets are currently flying above you?

How many offshore oil rigs are puncturing your seabed?

Who can lay claim to your minerals and, as humans often call then, resources?

What new sea battles do you anticipate?

How long do you give the lively presence of the Leafscale gulper shark in your waters before they become extinct?

What can we do to bring the fish known as the Common Skate back to your waters?

Where was the last time you saw Bas Jan Ader?

What new and, as yet, unprecedented weather is coming?

What wonders of yours will we never know about?

What are the signs that will herald the return of the Grey Whale?

How is this dialogue to be furthered?

Where does this situation leave us?

MARGARIDA MENDES

Sonic Blind Spots: Acoustic Research in the Lower Mississippi River

The engine repeats, the pump withdraws. We get sucked into discharge channels and trapped in backwaters. Radioactive dust on the horizon. Walls and ponds of waste get mixed in the water, corroding my fingerprints. Nitrogen levels peak, as the core samples glow. When we row, the waterline is subdued to a foam border, envisioned by ants as a nutritious conveyor of wealth. The intermixed canals of this chemical pond become the infrasonic rhythmic sites of industry's growth. Water shivers, water glows. In the mountainous intertidal range of cultivated dispossessed lands. Plantations gave place to petrochemical labyrinths for incarcerated souls. Swamp people, once marooned free, are now exposed to the ravaging control of uncertainty. The cicadas warm the air with their precious blues, inexhaustible tremors marking the mid-afternoon. As the season of termites sleeps, the crepuscule soon brings the howling dawn, and with it its cricketing hum — in the corners, in the marshes, in the mallows. The songs of a thousand frogs echo from below, attuned to the environment of encircling flows. The echo brings the gecko, the Mississippi in a thousand rows.

In 2019 I had the chance to visit the Lower Mississippi region twice, to carry out field work and partake in workshops around the region of New Orleans. I visited communities exposed to coastal erosion and increased industrial presence that stretched until the Gulf of Mexico. These journeys took place as I pursued my doctoral research at the Center for Research Architecture at Goldsmiths University, with a project titled "Sensorial Ecologies – Sonic Literacy and Restorative Listening in Watery Worlds." I used sound as an investigative media to document and engage with ecosystems under transformation, while carrying out interviews with activists, scientists and artists that I met along the way.

I joined the Augsburg University River Semester on the last leg of its journey traveling down the Mississippi from Baton Rouge to New Orleans. I pursued a project titled *Sounding the Mississippi*. I collected recordings of the petrochemical corridor soundscape, as I documented the lower Mississippi River as an acoustic space, using sound as a tool to environmentally sense my way into this ecosystem. I recorded sound with a hydrophone and zoom recorder microphone, both above and below the water line, as I canoed or whenever we had a stop on the riverbanks. In the end of the day I played back the recordings and had conversations about riverine noise and the transformations of its habitats, as I tried to make sense of the scale of extraction operating at site. By registering the exceedingly industrialized soundscape of the riverine embankments, and surrounding infrastructure, I studied the continuity between bodies and the environment. While searching for sonic residues of toxicity, I revisited my thoughts about the impermanence of matter and the mutability of the hydrocy-cle, reframing the river as living geological strata, and its surrounding riverine system as a complex metabolic site, where numerous transactions occur. I also inquired into how much is known about these ecosystems, and how much is left unregistered, untraceable, or out of the frame, and what tools, epistemological questionings or blind spots were left unanswered, and how these shaped or were the result of research practices.

~

Months after our journey, as I struggled to find any acoustic ecology research-er that had set their ears on this over-industrialized stretch of the Mississippi reaching the Gulf of Mexico, I still wondered how the disturbing omnipresent background noise was disregarded both by local inhabitants and by the scien-tific community. I set out to make a series of interviews on the topic, and my first encounter was with Natalia Sidorovskaia, a senior researcher at Univer-sity of Louisiana at Lafayette and one of the most experienced acousticians in the region, who conducted work in the Gulf monitoring oil drilling impacts in the cetacean community. She was intrigued by my intention to use sound as a tool to environmentally sense this stretch of the river, and how unprecedented cross-readings of water and atmospheric pollution across both human and oth-er-than-human entities could bring different perspectives about an ecosystem under distress.

I asked her and several other researchers if the infrastructural rhythms of Louisiana could leave a physical imprint on the bodies that inhabit it, whose vital expression seems to be endangered by the surrounding industry. Sidor-ovskaia told me that there is still much to study. Only few maps of pollution include electromagnetic properties in relation to soil geophysics. In terms of acoustic ecology, no maps exist of the petrochemical corridor. Everybody is fo-cused on the Gulf, where biodiversity is more representative, and not on the riv-er itself. According to Sidorovskaia, local scientific research on cetaceans could do much more to understand what acoustic communication is and how animals utilize it:

> We can detect species using acoustical signals, and do some prediction of abundance of population, we know we can use this acoustic database to understand the structure, genders, for example. But, as for recognizing individuals and understanding communication, I think these should be two immediate goals for marine mammals' future research.[1]

Sidorovskaia went on to speak about the impact that ocean noise makes on the species she has studied, acknowledging that the more subtle impacts of high baseline noise were left unregistered in her study. She and her colleagues noticed how cetaceans change their communication overtime as industrial noise grows, competing with industry by producing higher sounds to communicate with one another or to find prey. But the details of this adaptation remained unknown to the scientific team. This led her lab to inquire further into underwater sound signals by focusing for example on their reproductive utility among fish. According Sidorovskaia, acoustics is "everything" in the ocean:

> because there are no images in the ocean, they [the animals] cannot see. There's no light down there, so everything they know about the ocean is mostly smell and acoustics. That's their vision of the world. What they use is the kind of information they can extract based on the acoustic signals produced.[2]

If acoustics is the main medium for aquatic environmental assessment, then clearly my conversation with Sidorovskaia has pointed to several blind spots in scientific research directions. Most of the research conducted concerns ocean animals, and not the riverine and Delta communities, or other animals, and humans on land. There are considerable studies related to military industry and submarine use in coastal waters, with the first data reports from 1990, but no reports on the lower stretch of the river. Teams collect coastal acoustic baseline data and monitor the impact of oil drilling through acoustic surveys and through the study of whale behavior changes recorded in audiograms. However, their data cannot explain the absence of animals; it can only distinguish between the sizes of animals, particularly calves, through algorithms.

Sidorovskaia mentioned that the databanks are shared with NASA and SCRIPPS Institution of Oceanography. However, the datasets are endless and it is difficult to process all the material collected. And then there is the fact that incorporating these results in any kind of legislation would take decades. These blind spots in scientific research suggest possible reasons behind the erasure of the Delta and petrochemical corridor as an object of study: either lack of funding, or the omnipresence of the petrochemical industry in the area and its control over scientific research on the river. Much remains to be said about the evolutionary adaptation of species to the massive environmental changes that extraction and intensive agriculture brought to the Mississippi, let alone about how infrastructural and engineering investments have been altering the behavior of species.

> *How do we sense the environment and how does the environment sense us?*

Bernie Krauss' acoustic niche hypothesis speaks of animal adaptation to anthropogenic noise.[3] He predicts, that in a mature ecosystem, species will avoid competition by singing at unique bandwidths or pitches, and at different times. Therefore, no two species should sing simultaneously at the same frequency. The hypothesis moreover suggests that more mature ecosystems will exhibit pronounced partitioning of the sound spectrum while young or disturbed ecosystems will exhibit greater acoustic disorganization, with multiple species interfering in the same bandwidths. The degree of acoustic partitioning in a given soundscape is directly related to the habitat quality and biodiversity of that ecosystem.

This bioacoustics theory focuses on simultaneous spectrum occupation by different species, who lay territorial claims to several audio thresholds.

Acoustic biologist Mark Bee working upriver in the Mississippi studies similar phenomena, investigating what we can learn from the environment and ourselves by studying frog songs.[4] Bee speculates that we might find auditory solutions if we link back to an ancestor common to both modern-day fish and terrestrial vertebrates – amphibians, reptiles, birds, and mammals – who 400 million years ago might have developed a sense of hearing underwater. Bee's lab analyses frog responses to mating calls in spaces of high background noise density. His study has concluded that female frogs are less likely to find a mating partner and reproduce in noisy environments; noise constrains the spatial scale and extent of a female's ability to assess and compare different mates in a chorus. Frogs, like humans, explore similar auditory solutions. exploiting spatial separation as well as pitch differences to reach their listener. Hence reading a frog's response to an acoustic landscape could provide evidence about an environment and about the challenges that species face in adapting and reproducing. Much remains unknown about many other species' hearing mechanisms, despite the fact that anthropocentric noise is a pressing reality and that it occupies significant space in the frequency spectrum.

Bodies as sensors

(I am an oscillatory membrane)

The sky registers

What filtering organisms are accounted

The drift of the senses

Where does the nonhuman lie?

I went on to converse with Jordan Karubian, a biologist researching evolutionary ecology, animal behavior, and wetland conservation with a particular focus on birds and deforestation. Like Sidorovskaia, Karubian, too, was unaware of any soundmaps or acoustic ecology studies in Louisiana. I asked Karubian whether he has noticed any patterns among the species he studied regarding the ways they adapt to the course of present industrialization. He responded positively. Karubian had been surveying anthropogenic impact on ecosystems by combining genetic studies with information on how animal behavior diversity patterns have changed over time, particularly in the case of some birds. I was particularly interested if the region's industry left an electromagnetic imprint on the biosphere and atmosphere, thus altering species behavior. Karubian said that swarm behavior among birds in the Delta is an underexplored subject (with the exception of pigeon navigation that uses electromagnetic patterns). The other interviews I conducted did not offer any direct answers to this question, either.

Comparing various ecological patterns that drive evolution, Karubian studies bird species that contribute to seed dispersal and pollination. Tracking their behavior is crucial for ecosystem conservation. Birds are critical for plant reproduction, and hence they are structurally linked to the trophic chain and oxygen metabolization. Karubian told me that when "you do see a drop in the species that disperse the seeds, then you can see that the seeds are not being moved around as much, and then you can see that the seedlings, the next generations, are less genetically diverse and also more clustered in space."[5] This subsequently has profound implications for the surrounding ecosystem.

Knowing how extensively industrialized the petrochemical corridor has been raises the following question: how might industrially generated sonic emissions be destabilizing these seed dispersal and pollination processes and altering the region's ecosystemic metabolism as a result?. The proper concept of the river system is altered, for, if the margins of the river littoral are indeed fluctuating, as Brian Holmes predicted – not only aquatically, but also in terms of flora and fauna distribution – these are also constantly challenged by engineering implementations.[6]

I questioned Karubian how might the omnipresence of industry in the region and the resulting rise in background noise be altering species behavior and evolutionary adaptation to engineering incursions and man-made infrastructures. According to Karubian:

> Evolution is a process that in some ways that is similar to engineering. The process of evolution is one of change and refinement. In evolution, there is not this idea that things are getting better over long periods of evolutionary time but that, as environments change, life through evolution finds a way to solve problems and come to solutions. And that's what engineers do.

One can question how aware designers and engineers are to the needs of certain species, and to the functional constraints of a given ecosystem. Hence one must account for how adaptation and evolution links back to forms of knowledge production, worldview-making, and scientific ontologies. For, if the data collected and assembled produces particular forms of accessing the world and representing it, leading to particular infrastructural implementations and engineering investments, it also generates particular forms of environmental mediation. These forms of representation, which attempt to include other entities, are often unaware, as Sidorovskaia says, of alternate forms of viewing of the world. Sensing in the dark, they often fail. To begin with, scientific methods of study and how scientists survey an ecosystem are always anthropocentric and therefore extremely partial. Science's knowledge of other sensing systems is simply too scarce. Blind spots are endless.

~

Karubian referred me to associations working on restorative justice, who provide other forms of access to data monitorization in the region. LA Bucket Brigade, an activist collective running toxic tours and awareness campaigns around the "cancer alley" did provide alternative answers. LA Bucket Brigade conducts their own air sampling tests, equipping and capacitating communities by teaching them how to interpret data. The activist collective gives communities tools to constitute their own evidence towards gaining support from political leaders and public defenders. LA Bucket Brigade had a long and eventually unsuccessful fight against the construction of the NARCO chemical plant and directed all its present campaign efforts towards halting that of the FORMOSA plant. The ways they challenge the presence of oil infrastructure in the corridor have a fierce decolonial focus. Their toxic tour covered the 1811 slave revolt path as well as it called attention to the numerous petrochemical refineries; it made the connection between forms of resistance and extraction that Louisiana has witnessed.[7] Kate McIntosh, LA Bucket Brigade member, to whom I spoke mentioned that "If people's ancestors were able to fight slavery, we should fight petrochemicals."[8] McIntosh also mentioned that no activist collective or self-organized community movement was looking into noise as a permanent symptom of the extractive disruption at work in the corridor. The focus was on air and toxicity.

Our conversation revealed how the ripple effects of extractive projects operate at various speeds and through many modes of presence and are subjected to different thresholds of visibility.[9] A toxic event is dispersed, slow, and often cumulative, comprising countless metabolic mutations throughout an ecosystem. These mutations often escape existing regimes of representation as they unfold at different velocities across physical dimensions in an interscalar manner. The symptoms may be already evident in some cases, as oil leaks are visible and some cancerous diagnoses easily reached. But in many other cases, the legal battle against those harmed by extraction is based on an oppressive state of distrust and benefits from the temporal gap in the causal disarrangement between the toxic event and the visible evidence of the metabolic disruption of life. This legal battle is often ocular-centric and positivistic. It prioritizes what is visibly disrupted, altered, or diagnosed, marking a clear line across what is admissible as evidence. How might extraction's toxic impacts be differentiated otherwise? Might there be other ways of narrating, disassembling and reinterpreting the extractive event? Sound's relational quality as an investigative tool offers clues regarding how these questions may be addressed and reformulated, while also tapping into the blind spots of existing scientific research and politics.

Challenging the threshold of visibility and the primacy of the ocular, sonic tools reveal already existing power dimensions at play before they become fully legible as symptoms of extractive dispossession. Analyzing the politics of vibration, emission sources, and bandwidth use inequalities can reveal much about the colonial regime of extractive infrastructures by exposing the disassembled temporalities of the extractive event. The rise in background noise and chemical unbalance across the Lower Mississippi's ecosystem is linked with endocrinological and immunity disruptions. The sonic is both a symptom and a tool for surveying ecosystems under distress. One could analyze bodies' immersion in sonic networks by reflecting on different sensing processes and toxic regimes. This might be a form of the politics of the unseen and the unheard, that discloses numerous relations reassembled by the extractive event.

Why has noise as a symptom of extraction been excluded from the toxic equation for so long despite its omnipresence?

NOTES

1. Online interview conducted in October 2020.
2. Ibid.
3. Bernie Krause, "The Niche Hypothesis: A virtual symphony of animal sounds, the origins of musical expression and the health of habitats," published June 1993, consulted online https://www.researchgate.net/publication/269278107_The_Niche_Hypothesis_A_virtual_symphony_of_animal_sounds_the_origins_of_musical_expression_and_the_health_of_habitats
4. "Frogs, Acoustics, and The Future of Hearing: Mark Bee at TED x UMN," Oct 19, 2012. https://www.youtube.com/watch?v=mvCkrrfpPhc
5. Excerpts from online interview conducted with Jordan Karubian in October 2020.
6. Brian Holmes "Check my Pulse – the Anthropocene River in Reverse" https://www.anthropocene-curriculum.org/contribution/check-my-pulse published on August 28, 2020.
7. See artist Dread Scott's the Slave Rebellion Reenactment (2019), https://www.slave-revolt.com
8. Online interview conducted with Kate McIntosh on October 2020.
9. Rob Nixon has called "slow violence": a marked inattention to endured forms of ecosystemic and social vulnerability that have been set in place by corrosive modes of capitalist extraction, disempowerment and displacement. Nixon, R. (2013). *Slow violence and the environmentalism of the poor*. Harvard University Press.

MIGUEL BUENROSTRO

is a Tijuana-born artist and filmmaker based in Berlin. His work delves into the intersections of art and territory, emphasizing aural dimensions within a cinematic practice. His mediums include cinema and sonic interventions in public space. He is the initiator of *Cosmoaudiciones*, a sonic research project that reimagines the sound documents of ethnographic collections through collective listening, musical improvisation, and artistic dialogue. Buenrostro has showcased his work in the Biennale Architettura di Venezia, the Bauhaus Museum, Musée National de la RD Congo, Konsthall C, Stockholm, and Museo Casa Lago, CDMX. His films have been presented in various international film festivals, exhibitions, and public screenings.

WANDA CANTON

is passionate about abolitionist politics and the significance of musicking. She completed her PhD in 2025, critically examining concepts of the community and its capacity to reproduce forms of power and policing. She is the Founding Director of Sonic Rebellions, an international network of artists, activists and academics exploring the relationship between sound and social justice. She edits the Sonic Rebellions book series under Routledge. Wanda's other published works and presentations challenge the criminalization of rap music whilst championing the significance of rap and spoken word for recovery from trauma, drawing on her experience as a mental health practitioner.

REBECCA COLLINS

was an award-winning artist researcher working at the intersection between contemporary performance and sound. Her main research interests focused on listening, performance, sound studies, and creative/critical writing. Rebecca's practice addressed the dynamics of the sonic operating within specific environments and technologies, to explore methodologies of writing, making contemporary performance and sound art. Her first album *Stolen Voices* was shortlisted for a New Music Scotland Award in 2021. Her first book publication *Sonic Detection: A Polygraph*, co-authored with Johanna Linsley, is forthcoming with punctum books (2025). She was co-convenor of the Documenting Performance working group for Theatre and Performance Research Association (TaPRA). Since 2017 until her passing in 2024 she worked as Lecturer in Contemporary Art Theory at Edinburgh College of Art,

University of Edinburgh. In 2022 – 23 she was IFT's Artist-in-Residence, where she carried out the project Parameters for Understanding Uncertainty. For 2024 – 29 she was awarded a Ramón and Cajal Fellowship at the Spanish State Research Council working with the Visual Culture and History of Art Research Group at the Institute of History, Madrid.

HENRY IVRY

is Lecturer in 20th and 21st Century Literature in the School of Critical Studies at the University of Glasgow. His work sits at the intersection of sound and literary studies, the environmental humanities, and Black Studies. He is currently working on a monograph detailing the political, aesthetic, and acoustic life of infrastructure in African American literature.

NANNA HAUGE KRISTENSEN

is a Copenhagen-based anthropologist and audio creator working at the intersection of art, ethnography, and audio documentary. Her practice is grounded in a deep interest in themes of listening and loss. As both a maker and a listener, she is drawn to intimate, sensory, and open-ended explorations of human experience. Her audio pieces have been featured on BBC, Danish Radio, and other platforms, and have received numerous international awards. She is currently conducting a sound ethnographic project exploring the continuing bonds between the living and the dead.

BRANDON LABELLE

is an artist, writer and artistic director of The Listening Biennial. His work focuses on questions of agency, community, pirate culture, and poetics, which results in a range of collaborative and extra-institutional initiatives, including: Beyond Music Sound Festival (1998 – 2002), Surface Tension (2003 – 2008), Dirty Ear Forum (2013 – 22), The Imaginary Republic (2014 – 19), The Living School (2014 – 16), Oficina de Autonomia (2017 – pres), Communities in Movement (2019 – 23), among others. In 1995 he founded Errant Bodies Press, an independent publishing project. His publications include *Poetics of Listening* (2025), *Dreamtime X* (2022), *Acoustic Justice* (2021), *The Other Citizen* (2020), *Sonic Agency* (2018), *Lexicon of the Mouth* (2014), *Diary of an Imaginary Egyptian* (2012), *Acoustic Territories* (2010, 2019), and *Background Noise* (2006, 2015).

MARGARIDA MENDES

holds a PhD in Research Architecture by Goldsmiths University of London. She is a researcher, curator, artist, and educator, exploring the overlap between critical ecology, research methodologies, sound practices and ecopedagogy. She creates transdisciplinary forums, exhibitions and experiential works where alternative modes of education and sensing practices may catalyse political imagination and restorative action. She is a tutor in the GEO-Design Masters at the Design Academy Eindhoven and a member of Natural Contract Lab, a transdisciplinary collective of lawyers and artists working on restorative justice and nature rights across Europe.

SARA MIKOLAI

is a choreographer, dancer, interdisciplinary artist, and researcher based in Berlin and Sri Lanka. Her work activates sensory experiences through live performance, encompassing dance, performance, and sound. She also expands her explorations of dance into video, installation, and writing. Sara's artistic foundation is deeply rooted in her engagement with Bharatanatyam, which she has studied under her mother within the Tamil refugee-migrant community in Berlin since early childhood. Since 2015,

Sara's practice has evolved to explore dance through a listening practice, through which she examines the relationship between dance and music, movement and sound. Sara's work has been shown in various contexts, including The Venice Biennale (public program, Italian Pavilion), Tanztage Festival at Sophiensaele, Hamamnes at Wiener Festwochen & Kampnagel, The Listening Biennial, Australian Center for Contemporary Art / Liquid Architecture, Shakti Colombo Dance Platform, Gangwon Triennale, Le Alleanze dei Corpi Festival, Sa Manifattura Theatre, among others.

MHAMAD SAFA

is a London-based sound artist and architect whose work explores the intersection of multi-scalar spatial conditions and their sonic make-ups. His practice addresses the aural impacts of armed conflicts, shock and the aftermath of violence. He graduated from the Centre for Research Architecture at Goldsmiths University in 2019 and received his PhD in Law from the University of Westminster in 2024. He is an Associate Lecturer in Architecture and Media Studies at the Royal College of Art in London.

LUÍSA SANTOS

Ph.D in Culture Studies by the Humboldt & Viadrina School of Governance, in Berlin, and M.A. in Curating Contemporary Art by the Royal College of Art, in London, Luísa Santos is an Assistant Researcher, in Culture Studies / Artistic Studies, since 2016 at the Faculty of Human Sciences of the Universidade Católica Portuguesa. An independent curator since 2009, she conducted research in curatorial practices at the Konstfack, in Stockholm, in 2013; since 2019, she is a research fellow at The European School of Governance (EUSG), in Berlin; and, since 2023, she is a teaching fellow at the Europaeum, in Oxford. She is the artistic director of the 4Cs: from Conflict to Conviviality through Creativity and Culture, the Arctic Routes, Southern Ways, and the Institution(ing)s.

JAMES WEBB

was born in 1975 in Kimberley, South Africa, and lives in Stockholm, Sweden. His work has been described as exploring the nature of belief and dynamics of communication in our contemporary world, often using found objects, sound, and text to achieve these aims. To date, he has had solo exhibitions at the Art Institute of Chicago, USA; Yorkshire Sculpture Park, UK; Liljevalchs Konsthall, Sweden; Hordaland Kunstsenter and Kunsthuset Kabuso, Norway; and the Johannesburg Art Gallery, South Africa. Selected group exhibitions include the 8th and 16th Lyon Biennales, 13th Sharjah Biennale, 13th Havana Biennale, 4th Prospect Triennial of New Orleans, and the 55th Venice Biennale. His work is represented in several notable public and institutional collections, including the Art Institute of Chicago and Smithsonian National Museum of African Art, USA; Tate Modern, UK; MAXXI, Italy; the Khalid Shoman Foundation, Jordan; and the Kadist Foundation, France & USA.

THE LISTENING BIENNIAL READER
VOL 2: INFRALISTENING

Edited by Rebecca Collins & Brandon LaBelle
Published by Errant Bodies Press, Berlin / 2025
ISBN: 978–3–9827721–0–3

Design: fliegende Teilchen, Berlin
Print: druckhaus Köthen
Distribution: les presses du réel, Dijon /
DAP, New York

www.listeningbiennial.net
www.erranbodies.org